Energizers
and
Icebreakers

For All Ages and Stages

by

Elizabeth Sabrinsky Foster, Ed.D.

Printing (Last Digit)

9

Publisher—

Educational Media Corporation®
P.O. Box 21311
Minneapolis, MN 55421

Production editor—

Don L. Sorenson

Graphic design—

Earl Sorenson

Artwork—

Bill Johnson

Dedication

**To my children,
Tiffany and Christopher,
who continue to lovingly share their mother
with pen and paper.**

A special thank you to the teachers of Kitty Hawk School, who supported a new project and piloted many of the activities in this book. My wish for students would be that they have the good fortune to share learning with teachers, counselors and principals such as those at Kitty Hawk School, Kitty Hawk, North Carolina.

To my friend, supporter, and believer—Naomi... thank you.

About the Author

Elizabeth Foster has worked in a variety of roles in education as a state and national consultant, teacher, trainer, counselor, peer helper coordinator, curriculum supervisor, program developer, childbirth educator, and author.

She has contributed to the field of peer work as President of the North Carolina Peer Helper Association, as author of the highly successful student book *Tutoring: Learning by Helping*, and currently she serves on the Board of Directors of the National Peer Helper Association.

Elizabeth Foster completed her doctoral work at North Carolina State University where she focused her research on peer tutoring training models.

Dr. Foster makes her home in Manteo, North Carolina. She is currently employed with the Dare County Board of Education as the Elementary/Middle Level Supervisor.

About the Artist

Bill Johnson, a talented young artist, teacher, and coach, has captured the essence of energizing activities through his original pieces. A middle school art teacher, commercial artist, and private instructor, Bill explores movement through black and white contrast. Mr. Johnson makes his home in Nags Head, North Carolina.

Table of Contents

Preface

This book is intended to assist group leaders, teachers, counselors, and peer helpers in the development of relationships and active learning.

Learning has never occurred in a vacuum. The mind, spirit, and body unite together as a whole when purposeful learning takes place. For this to occur, the body must be alert, the mind must be acutely focused, and the spirit must be motivated to pursue the task at hand. With an infusion of energizers and icebreakers through classwork or groupwork, you can increase the opportunities for active participation.

Educational research points to the fact that increased time on task will increase academic success. In addition, there is sufficient research available to us today that suggests that spending a large amount of time focused on a particular topic or activity, without an opportunity for rest and refocusing through some stimulation, actually limits a person's ability to attend to the task.

The activities that you will find in this book are designed for all ages and stages. The variety of strategies provide a multitude of approaches to the goal of creating a warm, inviting, and exciting place in which to interact. Activities can be adapted to the particular number of persons or the ages of the individuals participating in your group.

There are some general guidelines to be followed which will insure increased success when carrying out these activities. Read through each and follow them for maximum results.

Guidelines

1. The leader should be prepared with all listed materials prior to the beginning of the activity.

2. The leader should read through the directions and practice, so that the activity will flow smoothly and fluidly.

3. The leader must exhibit enthusiasm for the activity to impart a feeling of excitement to group members.

4. All group members should be encouraged to participate with an open attitude. No one should be made to feel left out or inadequate in any way.

5. Be sure that directions are very clear to the members before beginning the activity. There is nothing worse than to begin an activity and find that halfway through no one really understands the directions. You may even wish to walk through the initial part of an activity to assure the understanding of the group.

6. Establish appropriate guidelines for the functioning of your group throughout the group's participation. Examples of some of these guidelines might include: not talking while another participant is sharing, not embarrassing any other participant in the group, no put-downs. Everyone's uniqueness is unique, and that is great!

7. Be sure to follow each activity with some type of closure or processing. In most cases, there are suggestions for questions or ways to assess the activity. It is important to remember that for each activity, there is a goal beyond having a good time and feeling good. Although you want all participants to have a good time and feel good, you also are attempting to establish an increase in the level of trust, relationship building, and sharing. Therefore, to assure that this is occurring and understood, it is necessary to provide time for the group participants to reflect on their activity and to

assess the success of the activity. Feel free to be as creative as you can in processing these activities. Please let me know of all the exciting ways you find to accomplish this task. I'd love to hear!

So just as a review - REMEMBER

1. Be prepared.
2. Be enthusiastic!
3. Make directions clear.
4. Provide guidelines.
5. Provide time for reflection.

Have fun! Good luck and stay energized!

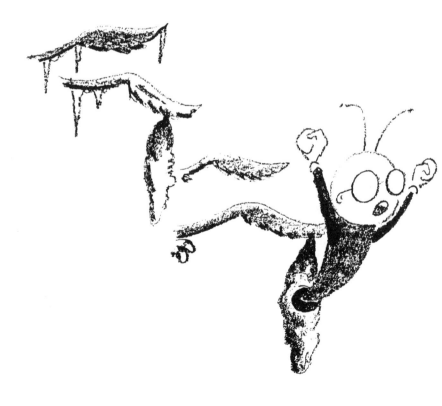

Chapter I
Icebreakers

Overview of Icebreakers

Icebreakers are often associated with terms such as "getting to know you activities," "warm-up activities," and "orientation activities." The purpose of an icebreaker is to help people feel more comfortable interacting in the group in which they are participating. This is done by learning about each other in a non-threatening way and by developing trust in and support for other group members.

Building trust and creating support is not something that happens in only one or two sessions. Therefore, be patient with your group as you try different activities in this section. Pay attention to the requirements of the activity to assess if your group is ready for that particular level of involvement. At the onset of group participation, it is recommended that you begin with low-risk types of interactions, building toward activities which encourage more involvement.

Touching is an important aspect of trust and support. The longer the group members work together, the more able they will be to touch comfortably. The group leader, teacher, counselor, or peer helper must first be comfortable with the activity and level of involvement before attempting to motivate others to become active participants.

Who should use icebreakers? Everyone!

There is no group, no classroom, no group session which should neglect the importance of using some type of icebreaker or warm up to establish a feeling of cohesion for the participants. A simple activity which begins with looking at our names is not quite so simple when it requires analyzing how we feel about ourselves and then sharing that information. This experience enables participants to not only look at their own individual meanings, but to see how others look at names or the characteristics associated with names.

It is important, during this phase of the experience, that goals for the class or the group be established and guidelines be provided for the successful working of the group. Though generally we use icebreakers and warm-up activities for the first several sessions of group work, you may use some of these activities at various times beyond the initial stages, so as to continue to get to know each other in a productive, yet personal way. The selection of the activities for this purpose is critical to the success of the goal.

Icebreakers are fun! Icebreakers are learning experiences. Icebreakers allow us to work together as people first and co-workers or learners second. We learn best when we are actively involved and feel comfortable in the environment in which we are assigned. Therefore, using a variety of icebreakers or warm-ups will help develop the kind of atmosphere which leads to comfort, security, and trust which, in turn, creates willing learners and participants!

Icebreaker 1.1

Amnesia Game

Number of People: Unlimited, however, this activity requires that the participants have worked together or have known each other for a period of time.

Materials: None

Time: 10 - 45 minutes. In a school this activity could be done during one entire class period or two people could do this each day for a short period of time.

Directions:

1. A participant is identified as suffering from amnesia. That person pretends not to know anything about the past.

2. The rest of the group tells some things that help the amnesia victim to remember and to become the same individual as before. The group should be specific, telling how the person typically behaved in certain situations. For example: (a) favorite words and expressions; (b) a usual way of acting in class; (c) a typical way of behaving around a teacher or adult; or (d) behavior in a certain situation.

3. The amnesia victim may ask questions of the group to gain more insight.

4. The amnesia victim might say, "What would I do in this case?" or "What did I do in a certain situation?" The victim might restate a situation that is known to one or more members in the group.

Discussion:

What are some of the things that most people remembered about the amnesia victim? Were these behaviors and actions pleasing or not? As individual amnesia victims, what 10 things come to mind that would remind each person what to do or how to be? How would each person like to be remembered? Some of these answers might be done on paper in small groups with a partner, depending on the age and the trust level of the group.

Icebreaker 1.2

Name Switching

Number of People: Unlimited

Materials: Name Tags, pencils or pens

Time: 10 minutes

Directions:

1. The participants should write their first and last names on their name tags.

2. The participants should pair up with people that they do not know and spend approximately two minutes telling each other about themselves—as much as each person can share in one minute.

3. When the group is notified that the time is up, the people in each pair exchange name tags. The participants now choose a different partner. This time they introduce themselves as the person whose name tag they are wearing, using all the information that was told to them by their previous partner.

4. Once again one minute is allowed for each person to give an introduction as the new person. At the conclusion of the sharing, the individuals in the current pairings again exchange name tags and again choose different partners. Repeat the process twice.

5. At the conclusion of the fourth sharing, stop the sharing and instruct the participants to find the person whose name tag they are wearing and introduce themselves to the person as if they were that person. Find out how much of the information was accurate and how much was lost in the sharing. Some people may have to wait while others are sharing.

6. Introductions can be made by the fourth name tag holder, introducing to the entire group the person whose name is being worn.

Icebreaker 1.3

People Scavenger Hunt

Number of People: Unlimited

Materials: People Scavenger Hunt List and pencil

Time: 10 minutes

Directions:

1. Hand out a People Scavenger Hunt List to each participant and explain the following rules.

2. Each person has 10 minutes to get the most signatures by each item on the list. No person can sign more than one time and no person can sign one's own list. Each signer must provide a short explanation or demonstration of the item.

3. At the end of 10 minutes, ask the participants to stop and to add up their own scores (one point per name, and one point per demonstration or explanation).

4. Recognize the high point participants and applaud their efforts.

5. Review each item by asking the participants to raise their hands if they signed or could have signed. Example: How many of you traveled to more than five cities? Which cities?

People Scavenger Hunt List

___ 1. Watches less than five hours of television each week. (How do you spend your time?) _____

___ 2. Dreams a lot at night. (Listen to a special one.) ___

___ 3. Gives great back rubs. (Get a sample.)

___ 4. Likes to sing. (Listen to a favorite song.)

___ 5. Has traveled to more than five cities. (Listen to a highlight.) List: _____

___ 6. Has never been on a diet. (Get the secret.) _____

___ 7. Likes to do adventuresome things. (Hear about some.) List: _____

___ 8. Has lived at least two other places. (Tell about the favorite.) List: _____

___ 9. Has met someone famous. (Find out who.) _____

___ 10. Has made an "A" in some subject. (List the subject.)

Icebreaker 1.4

Circlegram

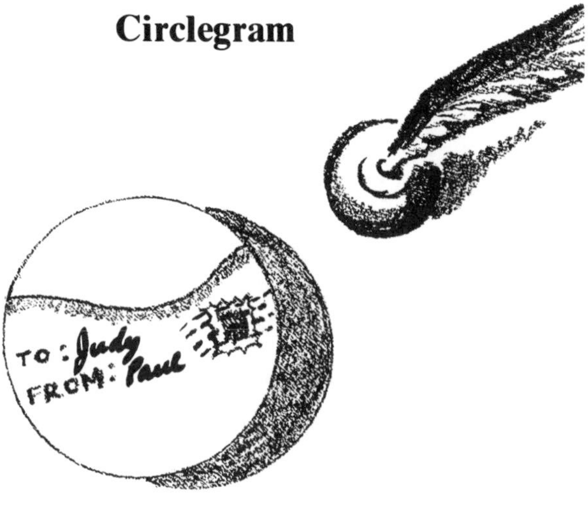

Number of People: Unlimited

Materials: Copy of the circlegram, pencil

Time: 15 minutes

Directions:

1. Look at the circlegram on the following page and note the different interest areas.

2. Tell the participants to pick the three areas that interest them the most and list them in a blank space on the circlegram sheet.

3. Look at each member in the group. Place each person's name in an interest category on the circlegram in an area which you think that person might have an interest or skill. One name may appear in several categories.

4. After filling out the circlegram, place a checkmark on the line above the circle for your top three interests.

5. The participants will sit in a circle and share information by beginning with the first person and having that person go through the circlegram, calling out the names of the people placed in the pie-shaped sections.

6. Participants listen and as they hear their names called, they are to place checkmarks above the categories to indicate that their names had been called.
7. Continue around the circle until all the people have shared their circlegrams.
8. Provide an opportunity for discussion on what was learned about people and what this information can tell us that would be most helpful. An offshoot of this discussion could deal with stereotypes and levels of involvement.

Circlegram

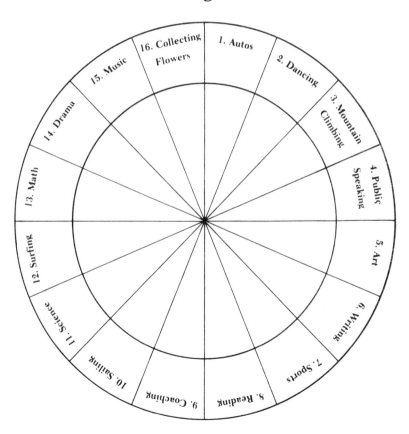

Icebreaker 1.5

All About You

Number of People: Unlimited

Materials: None

Time: 5 - 10 minutes

Directions:

1. Indicate to the group that this activity will provide an
   opportunity for them to look at information about the
   group members and to learn about each other. They
   should take note of who participates in each direction.

2. Make the following statements and ask the participants to respond.
   a. Everyone who is happy today, clap your hands.
   b. If you have brothers, blink your eyes.
   c. If you have sisters, stomp your feet.
   d. If you have a pet dog, raise your right hand.
   e. If you have a pet cat, raise your left hand.
   f. If you have a different kind of pet, raise both feet off the ground.
   g. If your favorite color is green, flap your arms like a chicken.
   h. If your favorite color is blue, cover your eyes.
   i. If your favorite color is red, oink like a pig.
   j. If your favorite color is purple, pull your ears.
   k. If you have a different favorite color, wave hello. (Ask what other colors are favorites of the group members.)
   l. If you like to play outside, click your fingers.
   m. If your favorite cartoon show is *The Smurfs*, hoot like an owl.
   n. If your favorite cartoon character is Spiderman or G.I. Joe, hop on your right leg.
   o. If your favorite cartoon character is Baby Muppets, Kermit, or Alf, hop on your left leg.
   p. If you have ever seen the television program *Mr. Rogers,* clap your hands over your head.
   q. Everyone who likes school, wink with one of your eyes.
   r. If you like to look at books, stand up.

3. Ask the participants, "From watching others in the group, what do you know about each other that you did not know before? What were some of the things in which everyone in the group responded? Why is it important to get to know each other?"

Getting to Know Your Smile

Number of People: Unlimited

Materials: 5 x 8 index cards, pens or pencils

Time: 15 minutes

Directions:

1. Pass out 5 x 8 index cards and ask the participants to place them on the table before them horizontally. Read the following instructions and pause after each item to allow them to complete the tasks.

2. Draw as big a circle as possible on the card without touching any of the sides.

3. Divide the circle in half with a vertical line.

4. In the upper left quadrant of the large circle, place another circle the size of a quarter, as in money.

5. In the upper right quadrant of the large circle, place another circle the size of a quarter.

6. Divide the card in half horizontally by placing a line from the left edge of the card to the first arc of the circle and stop. Do this on both sides.

7. Try to connect the outer points of the horizontal line by drawing a line to the top center of the card (middle).

8. Write the name you like to be called in the upper left quadrant of the card on the line that made a point.

9. In the first quarter-size circle, write your favorite color.

10. In the second quarter-size circle, write your favorite number.

11. If you could be any animal in the world, what would it be? Write it in the upper right hand quadrant of the card on the line that made a point.

12. If you could have any three wishes in the world, what would they be? Place the answer in the lower left hand quadrant of the card.

13. What one thing do you own that you would keep if you could have only one thing, following a disaster? Place that item in a triangle to be drawn in the center of the large circle.

14. Make a list of your three most positive assets. Place that list in the lower right hand quadrant.

15. Below your name, write what job you would like to have if you could hold any job in the world.

16. What one thing would you change about yourself if you could? Write it below your animal.

17. What makes you angry? Write this above your name.

18. Think of one thing that makes you happy. Write this inside a banana, placed on its side drawn underneath the small triangle. Nice to know you!

19. Having completed the above questions, assign group members to pairs or small groups to share their information.

Icebreaker 1.7

Hollywood

Number of People: Unlimited

Materials: 3 x 5 or 5 x 7 cards, pencils

Time: 10 minutes

Directions:

1. The participants should each be given one card.

2. Ask the participants to write their favorite movie on the top of their cards.

3. The participants are given five minutes to write the names of individuals in the group who also liked that movie; therefore, the participants should walk around asking people if they saw that movie and why they really liked it.

4. At the end of the five minutes, take a tally of the movie which appears to be the favorite of the group.

5. Variations can include favorite stars, favorite records, favorite artists, or favorite television programs.

Icebreaker 1.8

Relationship Icebreaker

Number of People: Unlimited

Materials: 3 x 5 cards (one per participant), Relationships List, pencil

Time: 10 - 15 minutes

Directions:

1. Ask the participants to select a movie, a book, or a television program with which they are familiar from the Relationship List.

    ### Relationship List
    1. The Turning Point
    2. The Odd Couple
    3. On Golden Pond
    4. Moby Dick
    5. Romeo and Juliet
    6. Heidi
    7. Old Yeller
    8. Kramer versus Kramer
    9. The Velveteen Rabbit
    10. The Three Musketeers

2. Continue with these instructions: "Write on the 3 x 5 card the selection that you have made. This selection should be a title that you reacted to, either because you really liked it or disliked it, or because it made you think about the people in the story."

3. "At the signal, leave your spot and find at least one other person with the same title card. There can be more than two people with the same title." (If for some reason a participant is without a partner, that person may select an alternate title and join that group.)

4. "Together, answer the following:
   a. What was the significant relationship in the title you selected?
   b. What propelled or moved the relationship forward in the story?
   c. Was it a positive (successful) or negative (unsuccessful) relationship?"

5. Allow approximately five minutes for the pairs to answer the questions, and about four minutes for random sharing.

6. Select different titles and draw conclusions from the titles that may be possible.

Discussion Questions:

What common characteristics were present in the various relationships? What was it that made the pairs or groups select the particular titles that they did?

Icebreaker 1.9
Magic Carpet Ride

Number of People: Unlimited

Materials: 6 - 8 carpet squares (optional) and 6 - 8 sheets of paper, pencils

Time: 15 minutes

Directions:

1. Place 4 - 8 carpet squares around the room with a time destination—a vacation spot or a favorite place—taped or pinned to each square. The number of carpet squares is dependent on the size of the group. If the group numbers about 10, the number of squares could be limited to 3 or 4. If the group numbers 30 - 40, then the number of squares should be increased to 6, 8, or 10. Items such as tagboard or construction paper can be used to substitute for real carpet squares.

2. Suggestions for magic carpet ride destinations include: Arabia; the Yukon in Alaska; Mt. Fuji; King Arthur's Court from the Knights of the Round Table; the wild, wild west in the days of Buffalo Bill Cody or Wild Bill Hickock; the undersea world of mermaids; an eagle's nest on top of a mountain; Tara—a plantation in the days of Southern ladies and gentlemen; the Great Wall

of China; the days of Queen Elizabeth and Shakespeare; Disney World; Plymouth Rock on the day the Pilgrims landed; the Star Wars era and a fight with Darth Vader; a NASA site ready to participate in a shuttle flight; Hollywood; the days of dinosaurs; a Beatles concert in 1965; a magical forest with Leprechauns, fairies, giants, and wizards; the Land of Oz to follow the Yellow Brick Road; the Never-Never-Land of Peter Pan where people never grow up; or the days of swashbucklers aboard a pirate ship. The list can be extended to other exciting places you might want to mention.

3. Tell the participants to go to the magic carpet that represents the destination to which they would like to go.

4. Once the groups are in place, a leader for each group should be selected that is willing to stay at that destination.

5. Groups should be given a sheet of paper to list all of the special reasons that their destination would be most appealing and exciting (much like a travelogue or travel brochure, trying to beckon tourists to their site).

6. Once the lists have been made, then group by group the designated reporter or leader for that group reads the reasons why that destination would be appealing to other members. If other group members choose to change destinations because the travelogue looks more interesting, they may do that at the conclusion of each group's report. The only person that can't move is the designated leader.

Discussion Topics:

What kinds of places were most exciting for the majority of people? How much movement took place? What can we get to know about each other from this activity? Did the leaders wish to move too? What were the most enticing descriptions? What kinds of descriptions were presented in a way most appealing to the majority? To what areas did groups not move? Why?

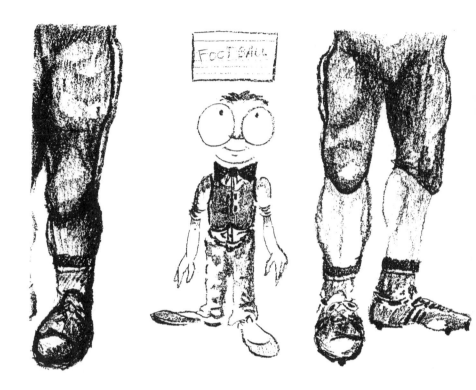

Icebreaker 1.10

Census Now

Number of People: Unlimited

Materials: 5 x 7 cards, tape, and pencils

Time: 10 - 15 minutes

Directions:

1. Using the 5 x 7 cards, list one interest area per card from the following and post the cards around the room: surfing; tennis; football; dancing; playing a musical instrument; singing, listening to records and tapes; going to movies; watching television; writing for pleasure; reading for pleasure; handicrafts; sewing; gardening; boating; fishing; drawing; working; driving; computers; video games; or shopping.

2. Ask the participants to walk around the room and look at the cards that are posted.

3. The participants are to initial the cards if they have an interest in that area. They may initial more than one card.

4. A group discussion can follow looking at how many people had similar or dissimilar interests. How many cards had no initials?

Variation:

Another idea is to put cards around the room with various occupations (good for intermediate to middle level students) or types of things they might be interested in doing as adults. Suggested topics for this: mechanic; beautician; doctor; teacher; lawyer; engineer; sales; truck driver; fisherman; gardener; farmer; veterinarian; seamstress; model; actor/actress; politician; dentist; carpenter; electrician; military service; or counselor. Include a large sheet that says "OTHER," instructing people to sign an occupation that may not be listed. Students could be encouraged to sign more than one or select only one.

Icebreaker 1.11
Sign Up Here

Number of People: Unlimited

Materials: 6 - 8 - 10 pieces of chart paper, tape, and pencils

Time: 10 - 15 minutes

Directions:

1. Put pieces of the chart paper around the room. Each chart should have a different topic of interest on it selected from the following list:

I like to study about space.
Gardening is a challenge to me.
Travelling in the U.S. and abroad would be exciting.
Making friends is an important part of my life.
My family is one of the things that makes me happy.
There are things that I would like to change in this school.
There are things that I would like to change in our community.
Males and females should make the same money for doing the same job.
The voting age should be moved from 18 to 21.

Topics can vary according to the age and interests of the group involved.

2. The participants should be instructed to walk around the room, looking at the different topics and signing their names on any of the sheets which represent topics in which they have an interest, making a comment on each sheet.

3. At the conclusion of the signing of the sheets, one person that has signed on each sheet should be asked to read the names of the people that have signed that sheet.

Discussion:

What interests do the group have? How many different interests are represented in the group? Which chart had the greatest interest? Which chart had the least interest? What does this say about the group as a whole? Does any particular pattern seem to be present? What comments are made?

Icebreaker 1.12
My Name Is Special Because...

Number of People: Unlimited

Materials: Paper and pencil, colored markers (optional)

Time: 10 minutes

Directions:

1. Each participant should be instructed to use one piece of paper and to write one's name on that paper in large letters. Each may choose to decorate, to outline, to draw pictures around, or to do anything that highlights any unusual characteristics or interesting quality relating to the name written.

2. On the bottom or back of the page, participants should write things that they like about their names, why their names are special to them, how they got their names, any nicknames that have come from those names, other things that they are called, and anything that they would like to add about their names.

3. Place people in groups of 4 or 5 and invite them to share information about their names.

4. Be sure to instruct the members of the group that they are to be active listeners, supportive of information that is important to others. Group members should use good listening and responding skills.

Icebreaker 1.13

Hometown Map

Number of People: 5 - 30

Materials: A large map of the geographic area in which the school is located.

Time: 15 - 20 minutes

Directions:

1. Provide a large map of the geographic area of the school, either a printed map or a hand prepared one, by including the locations of major areas of interest, major streets, and the school.

2. Ask participants to individually place an "X" and their initials by the approximate place where they live and tell about their home and what they do there.

Variation:

A variation of this could be smaller, paper-size maps, in which people would be sorted into groups of approximately four members each, with one map per group. Ask them to identify on the map where they live and share within that group information about their homes, families, and recreational activities.

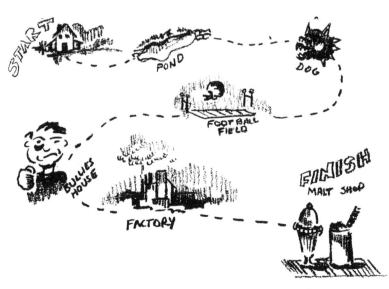

Icebreaker 1.14

Bouncing Information

Number of People: Unlimited

Materials: A ball that will bounce well.

Time: 10 minutes

Directions:

1. Ask one person to stand in the center of a circle and agree to be the ball bouncer.

2. As the person in the center bounces the ball to various individuals in the circle, those people have to tell something about themselves or something that they like to do. The people in the circle do not hold the ball more than five seconds; they bounce it back to the person in the center. The process goes quickly and a rhythm is established for the bouncing ball.

3. If the ball comes to someone who is not prepared to say something within five seconds, then that person goes to the center.

Icebreaker 1.15
Peer-O

Number of People: Unlimited

Materias: Peer-O Sheet, helping hand covers, and an empty shoebox

Time: 10 - 15 minutes

Directions:

1. Participants should all receive a copy of the PEER-O sheet and sufficient hands to cover their blocks.

2. Participants should be given approximately two minutes to walk around the room having other members in the group sign the empty blocks on their paper.

3. Members should not sign their names in a block more than once, unless there are not enough participants to cover the 25 squares.

4. As a name is called out, the person who's name is called must stand up, say something about their interests or background, and then sit. Following that, people would cover the name, if it is on their PEER-O sheet.

P E E R ·

Icebreaker 1.16

Fifteen Things I Love to Do

Number of People: Unlimited

Materials: Paper and pencils

Time: 10 minutes

Directions:

1. Direct the participants to draw a line down the middle of the paper, separating the paper in half.

2. On the left side of the paper, ask them to list 15 things in life they love to do. The participants should be encouraged to think as creatively and broadly as possible. Some participants may have a difficult time thinking of 15 items. It may help them if you suggest some things that people like to do in a variety of settings such as: indoors/outdoors; fall/winter/spring/summer; alone/with people; at school/at home; or entertainment/study.

3. After completing the list, the participants are asked to divide the right side of the paper into five narrow columns. "Each of the five narrow columns should be identified with the following symbols at the top: in the first column, place a $; in the second column, place an R; in the third column, place a U; in the fourth column, place an F; and in the fifth column, place a *."

4. "In the first column $, check any item which costs more than $5.00 each time it is done. In the second column R, check any item that involves risk. This risk could be emotional, spiritual or physical. In the third column U, check any item which you think others would consider unconventional or unusual. In the fourth column F, check any item that you think would not appear on your list five years from now. In the fifth column *, check your three most favorite activities on the list."

5. Divide the participants into groups of four and allow about 2-3 minutes for each person to talk about their lists. Ask them to compare the things they like to do and the different codes that they checked for these items.

Icebreaker 1.17
Nerf Bounce

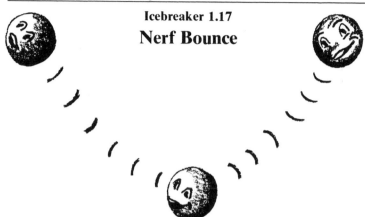

Number of People: 10 - 50

Materials: Chairs, a nerf ball or any other ball that will bounce

Time: 15 minutes

Directions:

1. Ask the participants to sit in a circle in chairs and ask one person to serve as the leader. The leader sits in the center of the group and holds the ball.

2. The leader bounces the ball to a member in the group.

3. Whoever receives the ball is to ask a question that would provide information about another member in the group. At this point the person with the ball does not know who is going to answer the question.

4. After the question is asked, the ball is bounced back to the leader in the center. The leader then picks someone to answer the question and bounces the ball to that person. The person receiving the ball is supposed to answer the question.

5. After answering, that person asks a question that someone in the group is to answer. The ball is bounced back to the leader who then bounces it to someone who will answer the question. The game is continued until everyone in the group has either asked or answered a question.

Icebreaker 1.18

Group Profile

Number of People: Unlimited (groups of 4 members)

Materials: Butcher paper, bulletin board paper, anything that can be used to draw upon, markers, and scissors

Time: 45 minutes

Directions:

1. Divide the class or group into smaller groups of 3 - 4 members each.

2. Select one person whose body will serve as the outline for the group project. Place the butcher paper on the floor and have that individual lie on the floor while another group member outlines the body.

3. The group then discusses the various areas of the body described below and comes to some agreement on how to represent them on the butcher paper:

   a. The top of the head - things to think about
   b. The eye area - things we like to see, i.e. movies, television
   c. The ear area - things we like to listen to, i.e. records, radio
   d. The mouth area - things we like to speak about
   e. The stomach area - things we like to eat
   f. The heart area - things we feel strongly about
   g. The shoulder area - problems young people may have to face
   h. The right hand - things we like to make
   i. The left hand - things we like to play or do
   j. The right foot - places we have been
   k. The left foot - places we would like to go
   l. The right thigh area - colors we like to wear
   m. The left thigh area - things that go thump in the night for you (what scares you)

4. After the groups have either written these things or cut out pictures or words to represent each area for the group, the smaller groups share their group projects with the larger group. Each smaller group selects a spokesperson for the reporting process.

Icebreaker 1.19

Make the Back the Sunny Side

Number of People: Unlimited

Materials: Newsprint or paper plates (1 per participant), crayons, tape, or pins

Time: 20 minutes

Directions:

1. Pass out a crayon, a pin, and a piece of newsprint or a paper plate to each individual. Use as many different colored crayons as possible so that people can identify which backs they have written on.

2. Have the participants form a circle with their right shoulders toward the center of the group.

3. Pin the newsprint or a paper plate on the back of the person in front of them.

4. Begin by writing something positive on the paper or paper plate about that person. Circulate around the group until each participant has written on everyone's back. Keep these sheets or plates for a time when the group needs a pick-me-up, and remember you can always say something positive about everyone.

Icebreaker 1.20

Adjective Match

Number of People: 10 - 35

Materials: None

Time: 10 minutes

Directions:

1. Have everyone sit or stand in a circle. Name someone as "It".

2. The first person begins by saying, "Hello, my name is 'Curious Christine' (as an example)," using an adjective that starts with the first initial of that person's first name.

3. This person continues by indicating to someone else in the group, saying, "And what's yours?"

4. The next person says, "Hi, Curious Christine, my name is Goofy George" and turns to the next person and says, "And what's yours?"

5. The third person says, "Hi, Goofy George, my name is Happy Harry." This person can then ask another person for a name or the person who is "it" can ask, "And who was that?" pointing to someone who has already been identified. In this case the whole group is supposed to repeat that name.

6. This activity goes on until everyone has been identified with an adjective and a name.

V — versatile
E — eager
R — racey
N — nice
O — open
N — noteworthy

Icebreaker 1.21

The Name Game

Number of People: Unlimited

Materials: Paper and pencil

Time: 10 minutes

Directions:

1. All participants should be given a sheet of paper.

2. The participants are asked to write their names on the left side of their papers with each letter being placed under the other, forming a vertical line.

   Example:
   L
   I
   Z

3. Group members are asked to think of words that describe them that start with each letter in their name and to write those words to the right of the letters.

   Example:
   L —ively
   I —nteresting
   Z —ealous

4. Following that activity, the group members share their descriptions by reading what they have written.

Icebreaker 1.22

The Clone Town

Number of People: Unlimited

Materials: One pattern of a face (frontal view), popsicle sticks, tape, scissors, pencils or crayons

Time: 15 minutes

Directions:

1. Tell your group that in this particular town, sadly, everyone looks the same.

2. Distribute a blank piece of paper and a popsicle stick to each person. Have pencils or crayons, tape, and scissors available to all. Pass around the facial pattern so each participant can trace the outline.

3. Tape the popsicle sticks to the back of the patterns after cutting out holes for the eyes and the outline of the clone face.

4. Have participants place the blank clone faces in front of their faces and walk around looking at each other for approximately 30 seconds.

5. Explain to the group that the only way to change the image of the clone is for the members to create some distinguishing characteristics that make each person a bit different.

6. Instruct the participants to draw on their cloned faces anything that they would like to make their person an individual.

7. After completing this portion of the activity, have the participants walk around the room, again looking at the faces.

8. Provide an opportunity for the members to discuss the differences and why people might not like to be all the same or why they might like it.

The Clone Town

Enlarge this pattern to life-size for your clone face.

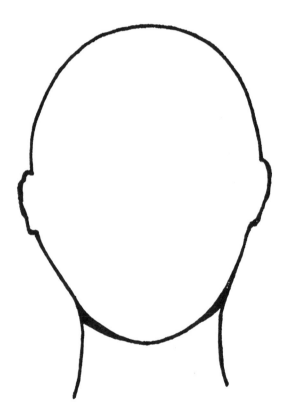

Icebreaker 1.23
Twenty Questions Interview

Number of People: Unlimited

Materials: None

Time: 5 - 10 minutes

Directions:

1. This activity can be used at the beginning of a new group to allow the participants to get to know the leader better. Participants may ask the leader any 20 questions that they would like. The leader designates the guidelines.

2. The group can have a few minutes to decide what questions they want to ask, or they can randomly ask questions until they have totaled 20.

3. The leader can summarize what was shared or the group members can summarize what was learned about their leader.

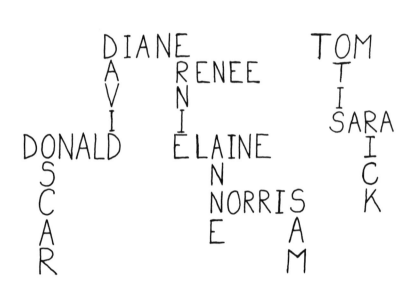

Icebreaker 1.24

Name Crostics

Number of People: Unlimited

Materials: Piece of paper and pencil

Time: 10 minutes

Directions:

1. Give a blank piece of paper to each person and ask them to write their names in the middle of their paper in block letters, about one half inch high.

2. When given the signal, the participants should move around the room, attaching others' names to their name if the letters fit. An example using the name "Carolyn Ann" follows:

```
            A                 T
            m                 o
C A R O L Y N           A N N
h       s     A n t h o n y
a       c     n         n
r       a     c         e
l       r     y         t
e                       t
S u s a n               e
```

3. The person who is able to attach the most names is the winner of this activity.

Icebreaker 1.25
Friends

Number of People: Unlimited

Materials: "Friends" sheet

Time: 10 - 15 minutes

Directions:

1. Remind the group members, "We all need to have friends and to be a friend. Sometimes it is interesting to look at the people we call on to help us in different situations, and to look at the people who call upon us for help in different situations. How about you?"

2. Ask the participants to fill out the "Friends Sheet" individually, then place the participants in groups of 4 - 5 people and ask them to share information regarding:

a. The number of different people on their sheets
b. The number of people who are the same sex or different
c. The number of people who are the same age, younger, or older
d. The number of people who are relatives
e. The number of times they included their parents on the list

3. Caution them not to reveal names if they prefer, so as not to embarrass anyone.

Friends

Who do you call on when:

1. You want to go to a movie?
2. You feel lonely and want company?
3. Your parents might be upset with you and you need someone with whom to talk?
4. You do something, and you want it to be seen or heard?
5. You need some special advice?
6. You want an honest opinion on your appearance?
7. You want to play tennis or swim or play ball?
8. You have gotten a new record and you want to listen to it?
9. You have a secret you want to share?

Who calls on you when:

1. He/She has a problem?
2. He/She needs special advice?

Who is the friend:

1. That will be a friend forever?
2. That needs you the most?
3. For whom you have a great deal of respect?

Icebreaker 1.26

Thoughts from the Past

Number of People: Unlimited

Materials: "Thoughts from the Past Sheet," pencils

Time: 10 - 15 minutes

Directions:

1. Hand out a copy of the "Thoughts from the Past Sheet" for every participant and provide approximately seven minutes to complete it. Observe the group to see if they finish earlier.

2. After pairing people to share their information, provide an opportunity for group discussion. This activity can be used about one month to two months into the school year, as an opportunity to reflect on changing attitudes and habits. It can be a good getting-to-know-you activity after you already think you know each other.

Thoughts from the Past Sheet

My favorite subject in school last year was _____,

but this year it is _____. Last year I always

enjoyed watching _____ on television, but this

year I watch _____. The biggest problem I had last

year was _____; now it is _____.

I used to wonder _____,

but now I know _____.

For years I worried about _____,

but now I know _____.

My biggest wish used to be _____; today it

is_____. Five years ago,

my best friend was _____; now it

is_____. My parents always

used to _____; now

they _____.

Icebreaker 1.27
Autographs

Number of People: 20 or more participants

Materials: Autograph Worksheet, pencils, small slips of paper with a number (consecutive 1-20 or more)

Time: 15 minutes

Directions:

1. All participants should receive a copy of the Autograph Worksheet.

2. All participants should place a number on their shirt front.

3. Participants will have two minutes to select the specific topics for which they will solicit autographs.

4. Each participant should look at the group members and decide who might like or be like the items below. Place the number of that individual on that particular line.

5. At the signal to begin, the participants will have approximately 10 minutes in which to accumulate their autographs. Ask the numbered individuals if they like or act like the item. If the answer is yes, then solicit an autograph.

6. The most successful person in the group is the one with the most autographs.

Autograph Worksheet

1. Thinks the President is doing a good job. _____
2. Born under my astrological sign _____.
3. Prefers to work alone _____.
4. Likes liver _____.
5. Reads poetry _____.
6. Looks attractive to me _____.
7. Has a male teacher _____.
8. Likes reading books _____.
9. Would enjoy adventure _____.
10. Believes in magic _____.
11. Enjoys gardening _____.
12. Is new to the school _____.
13. Appears to be friendly_____.
14. Likes to go the movies _____.
15. Loves computers _____.
16. Plays a musical instrument _____.
17. Likes to swim _____.
18. Enjoys competition _____.
19. Might be afraid of the dark _____.
20. Likes sports cars _____.
21. Makes friends easily _____.
22. Seems to be friendly _____.
23. Thinks school is important _____.
24. Finds music relaxing _____.
25. Would like to have a big family one day _____.

Icebreaker 1.28
Happy Grams

Number of People: Unlimited

Materials: A box

Time: 1 - 5 minutes

Directions:

1. Keep a Happy Gram post office box (could be a shoebox or another box) with a slit in it large enough for the "Happy Grams" to go through.

2. Cover the box with some colorful paper and make sure that it has a lid that will lift.

3. Provide a minute or two every couple of days for people to have "Happy Grams" read aloud to them.

4. Students should be encouraged to put a Happy Gram in the box to another participant anonymously with some message of thanks or praise or comment on something positive, in an effort to make sure that every participant receives a Happy Gram. The leader can participate as well.

Icebreaker 1.29

Today I Feel...

Number of People: Unlimited

Materials: A sheet with different feelings on them

Time: 5 minutes

Directions:

1. Pass sheets of paper out that have the following printed on them:

   I am happy. I am sick. I am good. I am beautiful. I'm a loser. I'm a winner. I am dumb. I am fine. I'm okay. I am bad. I am clumsy. I am a gossip. I'm neurotic. I am a bore. I'm a mess. I'm cool. I am successful. I am graceful. I'm a failure. I'm lovable. I'm slick. I am sad. I'm smart. I'm confused. I am a good teacher. I am a good person. I'm a slow learner. I'm not okay.

2. Ask the participants to circle the phrases or the sentences that describe how they see themselves today.

3. Have them analyze whether the items circled are basically positive or negative.

4. Ask them to look at one thing that may not be positive, and decide what they can do to change it tomorrow, so tomorrow they could circle a different feeling or statement.

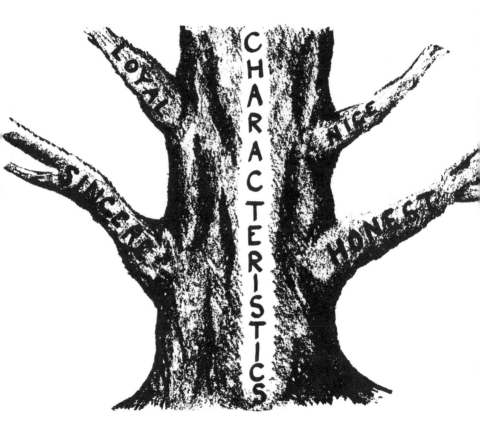

Icebreaker 1.30
Living Class Tree

Number of People: 5 - 50

Materials: Small post-it notes or tape and small 1" squares of paper

Time: 10 minutes

Directions:

1. Give the participants either several post-it notes or small squares of paper with tape.

2. Instruct the participants to write a positive characteristic on each square about someone in the room— without using any names.

3. Ask for a volunteer to stand in front of the group with arms stretched out on hips, simulating the post of a tree.

4. Ask the group to call out characteristics that they think make for a good helper, listener, or friend. As the characteristics are called out, anyone with those on their squares of paper should stick it on the living tree. You can decide if synonyms are acceptable.

5. At the conclusion of sticking characteristics on the tree, a summary can be made by the tree calling out all the characteristics of a positive helper, friend, or listener.

Icebreaker 1.31

People Package

Number of People: 5 - 30

Materials: Shoebox and items that participants bring to the session.

Time: 15-20 minutes

Directions:

1. This activity can be carried out only after the participants bring information about themselves from home. Instruct them to find a shoebox or similar size box and to fill it with items of memorabilia or things they find at home that would represent them, without using pictures.

2. Initial the lid or inside of the box so it can be identified later.

3. The boxes should be placed around the room and the participants given a few minutes to walk around without discussion, looking at the different boxes and their contents.

4. At the end of the silent viewing, each person is to select a box. (You could make a random assignment of boxes. Be sure the individuals do not get their own boxes.)

5. The participants are to review the contents of the box and write some description of this person based on what is in the box. If you wish, the participants can list any of the class members whose box they think they might have.

6. Following the writing of the description, the participants offer their descriptions. If they are correct, the person reclaims the box. If not, the box stays in the middle until the describer chooses the correct owner.

Icebreaker 1.32

Head Thoughts

Number of People: 1 - 100

Materials: Sheets of paper large enough to draw the size of a head; markers

Time: 10-20 minutes

Directions:

1. Pass out paper and markers and ask the participants to draw the shape of their head on the paper—lifesize.

2. Inside the shape of the head, the members should write or draw items that represent:

   a. things they like to think about
   b. things that they worry about
   c. things that make them happy
   d. people they like to think about
   e. places they like to think about
   f. subjects in school they enjoy

3. Have the participants tape the piece of paper to their chests with the head showing.

4. The participants should walk around the room looking at each other's heads with a marker, crayon, or pencil (something that won't stain clothes) in their hands. If they see something that they have written in their "head, " they should circle that item on the other person's sheet.

5. A variation of this activity would be: Hold the sheet in your hand. Walk around the room and look at the other sheets. Whenever you find someone else that has a similar item, circle that item on YOUR sheet. Another variation could be: When you see an item similar to yours, exchange heads and move along. It is necessary to look at the head closely. Call time after five minutes and have the members locate the original head they were holding.

6. Tally the number of circles in the class, or list the number of similar items and what some of those might be.

Icebreaker 1.33
Only the Shadow Knows

Number of People: Unlimited

Materials: Paper and pencil

Time: 10 - 15 minutes

Directions:

1. Inform the participants that the Shadow is an old radio character who solved mysteries. Have the participants make a list of 15 to 20 questions that they would like to ask of someone they do not know, which would represent information that would help them get to know that other person better.

2. Have the participants pair up by numbers, colors, or some method which would insure that the individuals did not know their partners.

3. Have the participants sit back to back with one person asking questions of the other, writing the answers. If at any time the person being interviewed wishes not to answer, the person replies, "Only The Shadow Knows."

4. Call time in about six minutes and reverse the process.

5. At the completion of the interview, the participants discuss the types of questions that they each asked and the things that were shared.

6. The participants select the information that they are willing to share with the larger group and introduce their partners.

7. Begin the introductions by saying, "Only The Shadow knows this information about Betsy, John, Tommy, and so forth." The partners decide what The Shadow knows.

Icebreaker 1.34

Body Profile

Number of People: Unlimited

Materials: Large pieces of white or brown butcher paper or anything that can be drawn upon - cut to body size (approx. 5 1/2 feet long per participant); markers; scissors

Time: 45 minutes

Directions:

1. Have each participant lie on the piece of paper, while someone traces the shape of the body. The body should then be cut out and can be drawn upon with hair, eyes, and so forth. (The actual drawing and cutting of the body shapes could be assigned at home and the shapes brought to class.)

2. The participants should be instructed to do the following:

   a. In the region of the head, write things that they like to think about.

   b. In the area of the hands and to the elbow, write things that they like to do with their hands and/or make with their hands.

   c. In the area of the heart, write those things about which they feel very strongly.

   d. In the right foot and right leg, places that they have visited in their lives that they enjoyed; and in the left foot and left leg, places they would like to visit.

3. An adaptation of the writing portion could be a homework assignment. Instead of writing, pictures from magazines or words from newspapers and magazines could be cut out and pasted on the parts of the body, particularly if this is done with younger participants.

4. Individuals should pair with another participant and share their body profiles, getting to know each other better by sharing the information from both.

5. If this is done early in the group, the participants can introduce their partners, sharing information about the partner by using the body profile.

Chapter II
Energizers

Overview of Energizers

What are energizers?

Energizers are generally short activities which are designed to stimulate thinking, to stimulate a group's interaction, or to spark motivation in an activity. Energizers can be used at the beginning of a group session or class, as well as in the middle or at the end. The use of the energizer depends on your purpose.

You may choose to create interest in an activity by beginning the group process with an energizer so as to stimulate thinking or to refocus the group's energy. An energizer may be used in the middle of a session as a transition from one activity to another or as a means of motivating students to greater participation if their interest and enthusiasm has waned.

An energizer can also be used to culminate a session by tying together the group's goals or to create enthusiasm for the concluding moments. Boredom can cause the learner or participant to lose focus of the goal for the activity.

Energizers are wonderful ways to build group cohesion and enthusiasm because they depend on the group's cooperation, participation, and interest to complete the activity.

Because energizers tend to involve people outside the typical chair and desk situation, certain guidelines for success should be considered by the leader of the activity. Having fun does not mean lack of control, discipline, or management. In fact, successful energizers require a thorough understanding of the group's guidelines to assure that all participants continue to respect the rights of others and do not lose focus of the overall purpose of the activity.

Suggested Guidelines

1. The leader must be thoroughly familiar with the necessary materials and have them prepared ahead of time.

2. The leader must understand the directions and be able to present directions in a clear and specific manner, outlining the steps of the activity in sequence to insure the group's understanding. It is suggested that the group practice the beginning of some of the activities to insure their understanding.

3. Guidelines for participation need to be specified *before* beginning an activity, not during or following. Enthusiasm will dampen if participants have to be stopped in the midst of an activity or have to be admonished following the end of an activity. If the leader prefers the participants not to run during movement activities or to maintain a particular level of noise, then it is only fair that the group know ahead of time what those expectations are.

4. Do not hesitate to repeat expectations prior to an activity, particularly at the beginning of group sessions or the beginning of a school year. This will add to the success of the group carrying out the activity in the manner in which you feel it can best be accomplished.

5. Be prepared for a certain level of noise when involvement occurs. If you are timid about this, practice with smaller numbers to become acclimated to this type of activity.

6. Energizers have a purpose beyond just feeling good. As you read through the different activities, it will become apparent that there are inherent goals in these activities, such as building self concept, building communication skills, or building interpersonal relationship skills. Processing the energizer in some way will be helpful in the group's understanding of those purposes. Without time to reflect in some fashion, you will

not be able to determine if the goals were met and the group will not be certain if they accomplished the goals. Following each activity there are suggested questions for participants/groups to explore. Other ways of processing the activities include visuals with transparencies, posters, collages, group reports, videos, and so forth. Your imagination is the only limit to the ways in which groups can reflect on their activities. Please adapt these activities and means of processing to your own needs and the needs of the group.

7. Remember that the age of the group, to a great extent, determines the type of directions that you give and the thoroughness of the repetition you provide. Working with primary students requires very thorough directions with a number of repetitions. Although directions must be clear for any group, the primary age child needs practice over and over in carrying out directions, so that it is clear and each child understands what is expected.

8. You are the key in every one of these activities. As the leader, you must be enthusiastic, be willing to be a participant, be willing to share, and be willing to risk some exposure. The leader must be a model of the expectations and be willing to guide the group towards those expectations in a warm, inviting, yet structured way. Structure in this case does not imply total confinement, but rather a structure which provides a *framework* within which the group should function. Identify the framework early, so that you, as the leader, are clear and the participants are clear about the expectations.

Growth is an interactive process. Engaging students and participants in activities which promote people interaction will enhance the growth of all those participating in your icebreakers and energizers!

Energizer 2.1

Spoon Marbles

Number of People: 10 - 50

Materials: Iced-tea spoons (long handles), teaspoons, tablespoons, and a bag of marbles

Time: 5 - 10 minutes

Directions:

1. This activity is set up as a relay. There should be a sufficient number of each type of spoons and marbles for each relay team. An obstacle course is set up over which each participant must travel carrying a marble in a spoon.

2. The participants are divided into an appropriate number of relay teams and lined up one behind the other. The first person in each team is given an iced-tea spoon. The second person in each team is given a teaspoon. The remaining people on each team are given tablespoons.

3. A marble is placed in each iced-tea spoon held by the first person on each team. At the start signal, the first person in each team is directed to carry the marble in the spoon as quickly as possible while running through the obstacle course to a destination and back to the second team member.

4. Should the marble be dropped, then the person returns to the beginning of the line and starts again.

5. When the member returns to the team, the marble is transferred to the next person's spoon without touching it and that person follows the same course, transferring the marble to the next person, until the team who is able to move one marble through all of the team members and the obstacle course first is the winner.

6. Variations can make this more difficult, including one hand behind the back, blindfolded with a hand carrier, moving backwards instead of frontwards, or alternating frontwards and backwards or sideways. More than one marble can also be used in each spoon.

Energizer 2.2

Family Photos

Number of People: Recommended for smaller groups of not more than 10 people per group

Materials: 3 x 5 index cards or similar size sheets of paper (optional camera)

Time: 15 - 20 minutes

Directions:

1. Inform the group that they will be assuming different roles from various kinds of families and they will be having their pictures taken. Families may include actual families, famous groups, or anything that can be portrayed in a family-like context such as:

   A family of polar bears in Alaska
   A family of farmers in Iowa
   A rock band playing in New York
   A family of orangutangs in Africa

A family in a kindergarten class
A school faculty/staff
The All-American family living in Dallas, Texas
The President of the United States and the Cabinet
A family of porpoises with their friends, the whales, in the ocean
A mixed family of birds: peacocks, buzzards, parakeets, and seagulls
A family of pine trees and mountains in Colorado
A family of grocery items in the refrigerator
A family of bees in a poppy patch
The solar system, including the Big and Little Dipper

2. Once the type of family is announced, they should write the name of their group on an index card and hold that in front of them, and assume the position that they would if they were a member of that family. Select roles most appropriate for the age of the group.

3. Either take a photo or pretend to take a photo as the different roles are assumed. This should be done very quickly with only 10-15 seconds between shots.

4. Approximately 5 different shots can be taken.If you actually take pictures, ask a member from another class, another teacher, or a volunteer to look at the pictures. Give that person the possible groupings and have that person try to identify the families in each photo.

Discussion questions:

1. As an orientation activity, what kinds of things can you learn about the group from watching this?

2. What kind of leadership emerges?

3. How were the roles defined for each family?

4. Who determined which people assumed which roles?

5. What is a family?

6. How many different kinds of families do we belong to?

7. How do roles change in a family?

Energizer 2.3
The Land Of...

Number of People: 20 or more

Materials: Slips of paper identifying the land and the characters

Time: 5 minutes

Directions:

1. Pass out slips of paper which contain different lands and the appropriate characters as people come into the room or when they are seated.

LANDS	CHARACTERS
Land of Oz	Scarecrow, Tin Man, Cowardly Lion
Land of Space	Sun, Jupiter, Venus
Land of Water	Shrimp, Tuna, Seahorses, Mermaid
Land of Never-Never Land	Captain Hook, Tinkerbell, Peter Pan
Land of Pinnochio	Gippetto, Cleo, Garibaldi, Jiminy Cricket
Land of Old King Cole	Queen, Cook, Maid, Blackbirds
Land of Goldilocks	Mama Bear, Papa Bear, Baby Bear
Land of Tara	Scarlet O'Hara, Rhett Butler, Melanie Wilkes

2. Ask the participants not to share their titles or ask others about their titles.

3. At the signal, the participants should mill around the room, person to person, trying to find others in their group, taking on the characteristics, assuming the accent, and modeling the behavior of the character on the slip.

4. The number of groups will depend upon the number of people. If there are 20 people, then plan for five groups. Groups should have four people per group; therefore the number of groups will be multiplied by that figure.

5. For each group, there is one person that has the name of the land that the other people are looking for; therefore, the land person should walk around identifying the name of the place and the members or characters should circulate trying to find the land to which they belong.

Energizer 2.4

Fried Eggs and Squash

Number of People: Unlimited

Materials: Slips of paper with different food items on it, box or bag, pencils

Time: 10 - 20 minutes

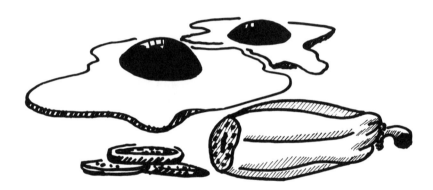

Directions:

1. This is an adaptation of the charades game. All items that are guessed are food items.

2. The participants should be divided into groups of four or five members per group.

3. A fish bowl, box, or bag should be prepared with slips of paper in it with various food items listed on them, such as: hot dogs, banana, fried squash, rice krispy cereal, apple, carrot, tomato, milk, soft drink - Coke, Dr. Pepper; potato chips, an ear of corn, spaghetti, pizza, soup, string beans, cookies, pretzels, apple pie, sunflower seeds, watermelon, popcorn, pancakes, fish, pork chops, sausage, bacon, potato, lettuce, doughnuts, cheese, peas, applesauce, broccoli, popsicles, peanut butter, jelly beans, glass of water.

4. The person selecting the slip, of course, can use no verbal signals, but can move or act out the food item that appears on the slip of paper.

5. The group able to guess the food items in the least amount of time is declared the winner. A timer should be appointed and 30 seconds noted as the limit for the group to guess the food item.

Comments:

Variations of charades could include types of animals, cities, types of clothing, names of cars, television programs, famous historical characters, special sports figures, names of nursery rhymes, favorite fairy tales, names of flowers or trees, or other special categories. If you use a variety of categories, consider this time saver for younger children: Paste a picture on a card or sheet of paper representing the category and then when the student receives the title, it would include a picture representative of the category.

Energizer 2.5

Touch Me

Number of People: Unlimited

Materials: None

Time: 5 - 10 minutes

Directions:

1. Seat the group members in a circle and give the following directions: "Half of the group will be divided from this point to this point." (Indicate which people will represent the different halves. The halves can change. There can be imaginary horizontal lines, vertical lines, or quarter lines. However, the circle is divided each time.)

2. "People on the right half are to get up and touch a piece of blue clothing on someone from the other half."

3. "People on the left side should touch someone with something in yellow."

4. "People on the right side touch something in black. Everyone sit down."

5. Then change the direction and say, "Everyone from the back half touch a shoelace."

6. "Everyone on the front half touch a white button."

7. "Everyone on the back half touch something silver."

8. "Everyone in the front half touch something orange. Everyone sit down."

9. Change the dividing line, dividing them into quadrants, and say: "The first quadrant touch only people in the third quadrant, and find someone with brown hair. The second quadrant to the fourth quadrant touch someone who is over five feet tall." (Depending on the age of the group, adjust this height.) "Everyone sit down."

10. "The fourth quadrant touch the second quadrant by finding someone who has pants. The third quadrant touch someone in the first quadrant who has a belt."

11. Add other special features as desired.

Energizer 2.6

I Cannot Say I

Number of People: Unlimited

Materials: Whistle

Time: 10 minutes

Directions:

1. Ask all participants to pair up and stand somewhere in the room.

2. Announce a topic for all participants to begin discussing at the signal. Choose any age-appropriate topic that the group might find interesting, such as: things I did on my summer vacation; why I believe in democracy; the most important person in my life.

3. The only limitation is that participants are not to use the words I, me, my, or mine in their discussions. If at any point a partner uses those words, that person is to sit down.

4. Blow a whistle every 20 to 30 seconds, at which time the participants are to change partners. If a participant's partner has already been seated because a personal pronoun was used, that participant waits until the whistle blows to find another partner, then proceeds with the discussion.

5. This continues until there is only one person standing.

Discussion:

Why is it difficult not to use those words? What kinds of things do we learn about ourselves from this activity?

Energizer 2.7
The Rabbit and the Carrot

Number of People: Unlimited

Materials: Chair, Cut-out carrot (or a real carrot)

Time: 10 - 15 minutes

Directions:

1. Choose one person to be the rabbit.

2. Have the rabbit sit in front of the other participants with the rabbit's back to the people.

3. Put the carrot behind the rabbit's back.

4. Someone is appointed to try to steal the carrot without being detected by the rabbit.

5. If the rabbit hears someone coming, the rabbit is to turn around and say "Stay out of my carrot patch."

6. Then, someone else tries to steal the carrot.

7. When someone finally succeeds in stealing the carrot, that person becomes the rabbit.

8. If the rabbit turns because of a false alarm, the rabbit changes position with another volunteer.

The Numbers Game

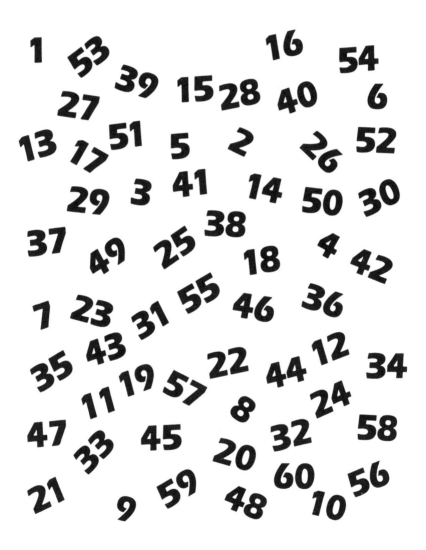

Energizer 2.8

The Numbers Game

Number of People: 8 - Unlimited

Materials: Number Sheet

Time: 10 minutes

Directions:

1. Distribute the numbers sheet face down, asking the participants not to look at it until everyone is ready.

2. When all participants have their sheets and are ready, state the following:

   a. Time will be kept on this activity.
   b. Turn the page over and put your pencil on No. 1.
   c. Your task is to draw a line connecting all the numbers in sequence.
   d. Draw a line to No. 2, it is okay to cross lines.
   e. Raise your hand when you are finished; now continue as fast as you can.

3. Begin timing and note the elapsed time when the first person finishes and also when the last one is through.

4. When all participants are finished, announce the completion times for the first and last person.

5. Ask the participants to pair up with another individual and to study the patterns. As soon as any pair recognizes some pattern to the numbers, that pair should raise their hands.

6. Give that pair an opportunity to demonstrate what pattern they see and then any others.

7. The following should be included:

   a. Odd numbers are on the left
   b. Even numbers are on the right
   c. The pattern moves down the page, then up, then down again.

8. The group can repeat this with a second sheet, comparing times.

Energizer 2.9
Mirror, Mirror on the Wall

Number of People: Unlimited

Materials: None

Time: 10 minutes

Directions:

1. Ask the participants to pair up and face each other.

2. One person is designated A, the other is B.

3. A assumes the role of the mirror and B initiates all movements.

4. A reflects all of B's movements and activities, including facial expressions while looking into the mirror.

5. B acts out some simple activity, such as getting ready for school in the morning in front of the mirror.

6. After approximately two minutes, call time and the roles are reversed.

7. As the pairs become comfortable, reverse the roles every 10 to 15 seconds. It should become unobservable as to who is the mirror and who is the actor.

Energizer 2.10
Ghost to Ghost

Number of People: Unlimited (will need an odd number)

Materials: Pattern of different colored ghosts for participants and pins

Time: 10 minutes

Directions:

1. You will need an odd number of people for this activity.

2. Have everyone pair up and the odd person stands in the center as the caller.

3. Pass out a packet of four ghosts to each participant (each a different color).

4. Have each participant tape or pin one ghost of each color on the body before any more directions are given.

5. Instruct the caller to call out pairs of colors to the group and the participants are to match each other's ghosts by touching the same color (for example, yellow to yellow). Yellow may be on one person's elbow and the other person's yellow ghost on the knee. In this case they would touch elbow to knee. Next color, pink to pink, and so on.

6. On the third or fourth color called, the caller yells "ghost to ghost" and everyone must switch partners.

7. People may not have the same partners at any time. The person without a partner is the next caller.

Adaptation:

For different holidays, use pumpkins, four-leaf clovers, Christmas trees, hearts, or turkeys. On the following page are four different patterns that can be used. Whatever is used is what is called out: Example—turkey to turkey, heart to heart, and so forth.

Note:

This is an adaptation of the energizer "People to People" for which no materials are needed. Body parts are called, such as arm to arm, knee to knee, and those are the parts of the body that touch.

Ghost to Ghost

Energizer 2.11

The Group Lap

Number of People: Unlimited

Materials: None

Time: 5 minutes

Directions:

1. The entire group should stand in a circle, shoulder to shoulder.

2. All members should then turn to the right.

3. At the count of 1 - 2 - 3, everyone is instructed to sit on the knees/lap of the person behind them.

4. If this is done too quickly, group members will fall over.

5. Caution members to move slowly and carefully to the lap.

6. After everyone is seated, suggest the group try walking in that position.

Energizer 2.12

Whistle While You Work

Number of People: 12 - 50

Materials: Slips of paper with names of nursery rhymes

Time: 5 - 8 minutes

Directions:

1. Depending on the number of people participating, select an appropriate number of nursery rhymes that can be whistled. As people come into the room, hand them a slip with a nursery rhyme on it, instructing them to not tell what is on the slip.

2. When given the signal, the participants should begin whistling the nursery rhyme on their slips until they find their group.

3. Everyone whistling the same nursery rhyme forms a group.

4. When everyone is in a group, the leader should direct the groups to begin humming their nursery rhyme and move around the room until other groups recognize their particular nursery rhyme.

Energizer 2.13

Puzzling Puzzles

Number of People: Unlimited

Materials: Duplicates of patterns of puzzle pictures or cardboard puzzles purchased from a local dime store.

Time: 10 - 15 minutes

Directions:

1. Puzzle pieces for each puzzle should be taken off of the puzzle and put in an envelope. There should be approximately 4-5 people per group, with each group receiving one puzzle and an envelope of pieces. Prior to giving the puzzle packages to the groups, one piece from each puzzle should be taken out and placed in a different group's envelope, which would insure that the puzzle could not be put together without the appropriate piece.

2. Pass out the puzzle pieces in the envelope.

3. Instruct the groups to wait until the signal to begin is given, and tell them that they should cooperate and put the puzzles together. The winning group will receive some surprise or token.

4. Once the signal is given, the participants should begin to put the puzzle together. As the participants begin to notice that they are missing a piece or have a piece that doesn't belong to them, they will begin to ask you what they should do? Where is their piece?

5. Continue to walk around observing the participants putting their pieces together. Do not respond or attempt to answer their questions.

6. The groups will generally proceed looking for their pieces, and will discover that another group has the necessary piece. The winning group is the first to put their puzzle together.

Puzzling Puzzles

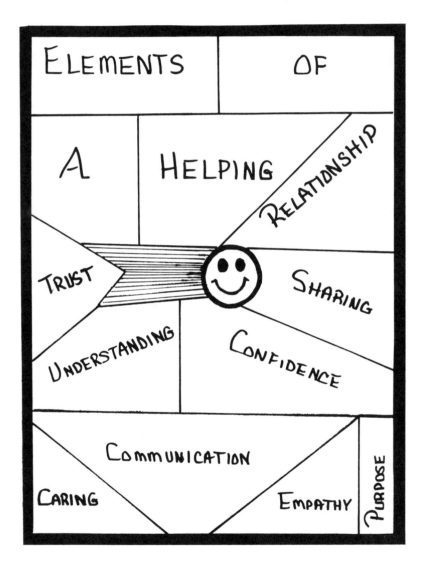

Energizer 2.14

The Human Knot

Number of People: Unlimited

Materials: Whistle

Time: 5 - 10 minutes

Directions:

1. The participants stand shoulder-to-shoulder in a circle, placing both hands in the center.

2. When the whistle blows, everyone is to grab the hands of someone else, being careful not to grab both hands of the same person, or the hands of an individual on the right or left.

3. Once everyone is connected, the object is to untangle the knot, without releasing the grip, except for permissible pivoting, as long as touch is maintained.

4. One pair will be instructed to release their grip.

5. Try to form a straight line.

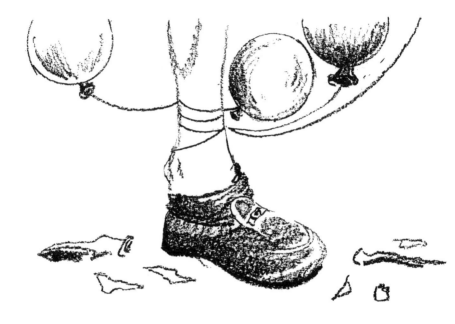

Energizer 2.15

String Balloons

Number of People: Unlimited

Materials: String, 10 - 12" balloons, and a whistle

Time: 10 - 15 minutes

Directions:

1. The Participants should be given pieces of 12" string and a balloon to blow up.

2. The string should be tied to the balloon and the other end tied to the right or left ankle.

3. After everyone has completed tying their balloons, the participants should be instructed to stand in a circle with their hands behind their backs, standing on one foot. It can be either foot.

4. When the whistle blows, the group moves around each person, trying to pop someone else's balloon.

5. Once a balloon is popped, that person sits down.

6. The winner is the last person with the balloon still inflated and attached to the ankle.

Energizer 2.16

The Glob

Number of People: Unlimited

Materials: Pieces of masking or scotch tape (enough for each participant to have 5 pieces of tape)

Time: 5 - 10 minutes

Directions:

1. Instruct the participants to roll pieces of tape so that they will stick to the body in five different places.

2. Have the members form a circle and pair up with someone else.

3. Call out the word "stick" and the partners choose one piece of tape on each other and stick those two pieces of tape together, bodies and tape sticking. They should then walk around the room in that position for 10 seconds. Call time.

4. Call out "stick" and the pairs move to another pair, making a group of four, sticking in two new places. The four members will move about the room for 10 seconds until time is called.

5. Following that, call "stick" again, and four people move until all five pieces of tape have been stuck so that the group becomes a glob.

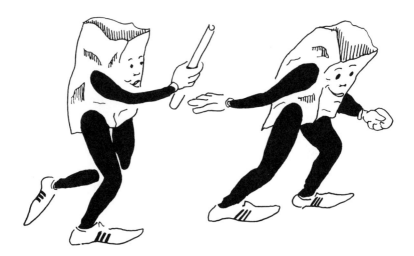

Energizer 2.17

Paper Bag Relay

Number of People: 10 - 50

Time: 10 minutes

Directions:

1. Divide the groups into teams of six each.
2. Instruct the teams to line up one behind the other.
3. The first two people form the first pair in each team. One person places a bag over the head of the partner.
4. Partners are to race with the leader, holding the hand of the paper-bagged person, taking that person to a pivotal point and returning back to the team, giving the bag to the next set of partners, until all six people have had the bag on their head.
5. The winning team is the team who returns back first.
6. HINT—setting up some type of obstacle course makes it more interesting. Be sure to caution members to protect the bagged partners.

Energizer 2.18

Help

Number of People: Unlimited

Materials: None

Time: 2 minutes

Directions:

1. Tell the participants that they are going to be given a word which is associated with peer work or students helping students, and as soon as they hear the word as a full group, they are to spell it out by standing in a position so that the letters are recognizable.

2. Leader calls out the word "help!"

3. People get into that position and spell the word with an exclamation mark!

4. Other words that can be used: care, share, love, grow, peer, or hand.

Energizer 2.19
Silent Moves

Time: 10 - 30

Materials: Available in most classrooms

Time: 10 minutes

Directions:

1. Divide the group in half.

2. Ask each of the groups to get into pairs.

3. Provide one person in each pair with a direction that they are to give their partner. There will be approximately 4 or 5 items to retrieve. The direction states the item to retrieve and the approximate location in the room of the object.

4. This direction is asking them to go somewhere in the classroom and bring back a particular object to them. Suggestions for items to bring back would include: an eraser, pencil, piece of chalk, crayon, piece of paper, ruler, plant—anything that is light and unbreakable.

5. This message cannot be shown to the partner or shared verbally. The message must be conveyed by standing in the same position and using silent messages.

6. The team whose partners are able to bring back all of the items first wins.

7. Signal the start.

Energizer 2.20

Shmoo and Aardvark Game

Number of People: 5 - 50

Materials: An object for the shmoo and an object for the aardvark

Time: 10 minutes

Directions:

1. The large group should be divided into two or more smaller groups with equal members of 5 to 10.

2. Each small group should form its own circle and the participants select two small objects that can easily be passed around the circle (i.e. comb, pen, shoe, ring).

3. One object should be designated the shmoo and the other object should be designated the aardvark. One participant in each group should be chosen to be the leader (A). The leader holds the shmoo and aardvark until told to begin.

4. When the groups are told to start, A turns to the person B on the right and says, "This is a shmoo."

5. B responds by saying, "A what?" A repeats, "A shmoo" and passes the shmoo to B.

6. B then turns to the person C on the right and says, "This is a shmoo." C responds to B by asking, "A what?" B than asks A, "What?" A responds to B saying, "A shmoo."

7. B makes the same response to C and passes the shmoo to D. C repeats this procedure with the person D on the right.

8. Each time the question, "A what?" must be passed by each participant until it comes back to A. A must in turn begin passing the statement "A shmoo" each time.

9. This procedure continues until the shmoo is passed counter clockwise around the group back to A.

10. After passing the shmoo to B, A turns to the person (1) on the left and says, "This is an aardvark." The aardvark is passed clockwise around the circle, using the same procedure as with the shmoo.

11. The small group that passes both its shmoo and aardvark completely around first wins. If the group gets confused, they have to start from the beginning in order to compete.

Energizer 2.21

Cooperation Squares

Number of People: Unlimited

Materials: Squares of paper with one letter per square spelling Cooperation

Time: 5 minutes

Directions:

1. Provide enough sets of the paper squares for each group. Have approximately three to five members per group. Pass out envelopes with the squares inside. Each square has a letter which, when placed together, spells C O O P E R A T I O N.

2. Tell the participants to begin sorting the squares when given the signal.

3. The groups are to put the squares in sequence so that a word is spelled which is associated with helping.

4. The first group who is able to unscramble the squares and spell "cooperation" wins.

BOWS IN HAIR

Birthdays in November

RED HAIR

PLAY SOCCER

READ BOOKS

Fish

Draw Pictures

Energizer 2.22

I Like People, But Especially...

Number of People: Unlimited

Materials: None

Time: 10 minutes

Directions:

1. The participants form a circle, sitting on chairs.

2. Appoint a leader. Take the leader's chair out of the circle.

3. The leader stands in the center of the circle and announces: "I like everybody here, but I especially like those people who... (then names items of clothing, appearance, age, and so forth that pertain to participants)." Examples: have red hair, wear blue jeans, have red socks, know how to read, have birthdays in October, are 15 years old, like to play sports.

4. Everyone to whom this message pertains must find a new chair at the same time the leader tries to get a chair.

5. Whoever is left without a chair repeats the process.

6. No one may sit in the same chair once it has been vacated.

Energizer 2.23

Fourplay

Number of People: Unlimited (groups of four)

Materials: None

Time: 10 minutes

Directions:

1. Four players comprising a team may compete.

2. The members of the team should sit down with their backs together.

3. Without using their hands, the members must stand up, run across the room and back around any designated course, and return to their original sitting position, continuing at all times to keep their backs together.

4. Teams can compete against each other or be timed and compete against their own time.

Energizer 2.24
Blooie

Number of People: Unlimited

Materials: None

Time: 10 minutes

Directions:

1. The participants should form a circle, sitting on chairs.
2. If names are unknown, then name tags should be worn.
3. Stand in the center of the circle and give the following instructions: "I will pick a person in the circle to be "it" and ask "it"—"Who do you want for your friends?" The "it" person then responds in one of two ways: two people (other than the persons sitting on each side) can be named. If two people are named correctly, then those two people and the two next to the person who is "it" must change seats as the leader in the center of the circle attempts to get a seat. Thus five people are vying for four chairs.
4. If the "it" person says blooie (as the second option), everyone in the group must move at least two chairs from where they were. Whoever is left without a chair gets in the center of the circle, is the leader, and repeats the process.

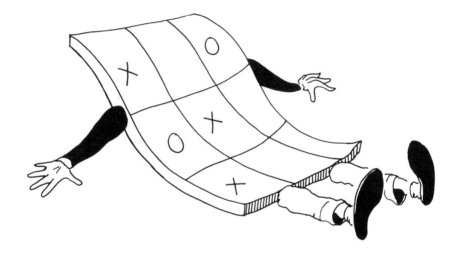

Energizer 2.25

Human Tic Tac Toe

Number of People: 10 - 50

Materials: Tape, paper

Time: 10 minutes

Directions:

1. Place a human sized tic-tac-toe board on the floor with masking tape. This could be done outside with chalk.

2. Divide participants into groups of five or six.

3. Half of the groups should be designated "X's" and half should be designated as "O's". Members should place signs on their shirts with the designated team sign.

4. There have to be even numbers of groups for Tic Tac Toe to work.

5. There should be one leader assigned to each group who is the player for the team, and play proceeds with tic tac toe by placing bodies in the squares.

6. The leader decides where to place the bodies.

7. People are placed in the appropriate place and run-offs can be played with the team with the most wins being declared the winner.

Energizer 2.26

Feeling Rumors

Number of People: 10 - 30

Materials: None

Time: 5 - 10 minutes

Directions:

1. Everyone should be seated in a circle with their right shoulders facing the inside of the circle. Therefore, everyone is facing someone's back.

2. One person is designated to share a feeling with the person in front.

3. The group should be asked to keep their eyes lowered or covered or closed so as not to see the feeling that is being passed.

4. Each person can tap the shoulder of the person in front to whom the feeling is passed, and that person can turn around and look then.

5. The object is to see if the facial expression or the intent of the original leader is salvaged at the end of the passing.

Energizer 2.27

Music Moods

Number of People: Unlimited

Materials: Music (records or tapes of varying tempos)

Time: 10 minutes

Directions:

1. Select a leader for the activity.

2. Have a variety of types of music that can be switched from one to the next quickly. Preparing a tape ahead of time would make this easier.

3. The leader is to instruct the group to carry out various types of movements. Examples: skip, walk, hop. They should carry out those particular types of movement when instructed according to the beat or tempo of the music, as it makes them feel.

Energizer 2.28

Simon Says

Number of People: Unlimited

Materials: None

Time: 5 - 10 minutes

Directions:

1. A leader stands in front of the rest of the group that is also standing. This activity is similar to the children's game, Simon Says, as it can be used at the beginning of any session, in the middle, or at the end to liven up the group.

2. The leader gives directions, such as: "Simon says, put your hands on your head"—the group follows.

3. The leader may say, "Put your hands on your hips." Group members are not to make any move unless Simon Says; therefore, if anyone puts hands on hips, that person or individual sits down.

4. After two minutes of that portion, switch to: "Simon says, listen to Mary" and then Mary gives 4 or 5 directions and then says, "Simon says listen to John" and so on, so that each group member gets a chance to be Simon.

Energizer 2.29
What's the Scarf?

Number of People: 10 - 30

Materials: Some type of headscarf or handkerchief

Time: 10 minutes

Directions:

1. Have the participants sit in a circle.

2. Begin by explaining that the scarf being held is not really a scarf. It really is a bracelet. Wrap it around your wrist to demonstrate that it can take on some other function or appearance.

3. Designate the next person to think of something different that the scarf can be and the scarf moves from person to person around the room.

4. The group is to guess the function of the scarf.

5. There can be no verbal hints.

6. The group must successfully guess before the scarf can move on.

7. Some uses of the scarf may require the participant to get up from the chair.

8. The group should guess while the scarf goes around the circle about three times.

Energizer 2.30

Balloon Relay

Number of People: Unlimited

Materials: 2 - 5 balloons

Time: 5 - 10 minutes

Directions:

1. Separate the participants into groups of six members each, unless the class is small, then make the groups smaller.

2. The object for each group is to go to a designated place while bouncing a balloon in the air and returning it to another team member as part of a relay.

3. Prior to the relay, designate to what point the balloon is to be bounced and then returned to each group member.

4. The group who is able to bounce the balloon in the air without it touching the floor or any other object is the winner.

5. If the balloon touches the floor, that group member must return to the starting point and begin again.

Energizer 2.31

Machines

Number of People: 10 - 20

Materials: None

Time: 7 - 10 minutes

Directions:

1. Ask the participants to stand shoulder to shoulder in a straight line.

2. Individuals are to think of a machine movement that they will initiate once they are touched on their right.

3. Give the signal and indicate that the first person in the row should touch the person to the left, which is the indicator for that person to begin, and so on down the line until the last person begins moving; so you have one large machine.

4. Now ask each of the machines to think of a sound to put with its movement.

5. The same process is repeated, this time with a stationary movement and a sound.

6. You can add a movement away from the line for a third go-around, so the movement is about the room with sound; however, each part of the machine must touch the next person for that machine to begin.

Energizer 2.32

Animal Friends

Number of People: 12 - 50

Materials: Marker, paper, and tape

Time: 15 minutes

Directions:

1. Give each participant a piece of paper and a marker.

2. Ask them to write the name of the animal they would like to be. Write in large letters.

3. Next, ask the participants to tape the papers on the front of their chests with the name facing them, so no one can see what has been written.

4. Now the fun begins! Everyone is to begin acting out and/or sounding out the animal written on the paper.

5. All animals should pay attention to the sounds that become familiar and seek partners or groups of like animals. If a dog hears another dog barking, then the dog should move closer to that dog. Turn the sign, and if it is the same, stay together looking for others.

6. If there is a person who has no one else like the named animal, then that participant should join in with a group whose animal seems most closely related or one who would be an ally.

7. After everyone is in a newly formed group, they should now move around as a group, acting as they would react to their animal's enemies. For example, a dog would bark at a cat—maybe chase it. A cat might try to snatch a bird. Have fun!

8. This continues until you have observed the group take on individual and group characteristics; provide time for discussion.

Energizer 2.33
Taxi Jam

Number of People: Unlimited

Materials: Slips of paper with "Beep Beep" (car) or "Honk Honk" (car) or Vroom (truck) or Zoom (motorcycle)

Time: 5 - 10 minutes

Directions:

1. Pass out slips of paper to all participants. The slips will say either "Beep Beep," "Vroom," or "Honk Honk" and only one will say "Zoom" (motorcycle).

2. Tell the participants to keep the identity of their slips private.

3. Have the participants spread out in all parts of the room, filling corners, the center, and so forth.

4. Select one person to be the driver who can move through the taxi jam/traffic jam and that person goes to any individual in the room saying "beep beep" or "honk honk," whichever is on the slip. That person is able to move with the first person, making the sound on the slip, and they move together, hands placed in the driving position with shoulders touching as they move along, repeating their sound, trying to find the motorcycle, who can free up the entire traffic jam.

5. No other cars can move without being touched.

6. Once the motorcycle is found, it can zoom throughout the room, touching the remaining vehicles, freeing up the traffic jam.

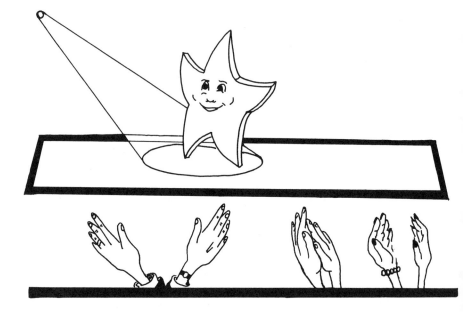

Energizer 2.34

Applause

Number of People: Unlimited

Materials: None (Star, optional)

Time: 5 - 12 minutes

Directions:

1. Ask for a volunteer to leave the room while instructions are given to the group.

2. The group is to select one person who will be the star. That is the person who the volunteer will be looking for upon returning to the room.

3. The participants are to spread themselves around the room, either on chairs or on the floor, covering as much space as possible.

4. When the volunteer returns, the volunteer should move from person to person trying to locate the star.

5. The clue to whether the volunteer is getting closer will be by the applause that the group provides as the volunteer gets closer and closer to the star.

6. If the volunteer is cold and moves away, then the clapping should decrease or cease.

7. As soon as the star is found, a real star can be flashed (made out of construction paper or tagboard). Then the star leaves the room and the group selects another star.

Energizer 2.35
Who's the Leader?

Number of People: Unlimited

Materials: None

Time: 10 minutes

Directions:

1. Ask a volunteer to leave the room for the group to receive instructions.

2. The group is told that they are to select a leader who will initiate different sounds or movements while they are sitting or standing in a circle.

3. The group should attempt to pick up the movement without looking directly at the leader, so as to fool the volunteer whose objective it is to find the leader.

4. The individual returns to the circle and stands in the middle.

5. Everyone, except the person in the middle, knows who the leader is. The group should initiate the action, predetermined, as the volunteer enters the room. The leader must change movements at least every 30 seconds. A timer could be appointed if necessary.

6. The volunteer has a maximum time of one minute between guesses and a maximum of three guesses to find the leader.

7. If successful, then the leader changes places with the volunteer.

8. The volunteer at this point can turn around or again leave the room to designate who the next leader is.

9. This continues until five or six different leaders have successfully fooled the volunteer.

Energizer 2.36
Don't Fool Mother Nature

Number of People: 20 - 50

Materials: Cards with seasons on them

Time: 10 - 20 minutes

Directions:

1. Divide the participants into two groups.

2. One group will be "seasons" and the other group will be "weather conditions." Seasons to be used: fall; winter, spring; summer; and free season. Weather conditions to be used: sunny day, tornado; thunderstorm; hurricane; and breezy cloudy day.

3. The "seasons" group is to make signs with the season they select. These signs can be hung around their necks or taped to their shirts. Every member should hold a season. They will be duplicated. Use only ONE free season. Have the words face inward, towards the chest.

4. The weather group is to select the type of weather from the list and place that weather on a card to hold. Each member will have a weather condition. They will be repeated. Have the words face inward, towards the chest.

5. The object is to gain as many players on your side as possible. This won't be known until time is called.

6. When the signal to begin is given, each member of the weather conditions group approaches a seasons person, stating the condition. One is stronger than the other. Whichever person wins then moves on to another pair, approaching them with the condition or season that won until time is called. Listed below are the strength areas:

THUNDERSTORM beats summer and spring, but not winter, fall, or free
TORNADO beats all seasons except free season
HURRICANE beats summer and fall, but not winter, spring, or free
SUNNY DAY beats winter and fall, but not spring, summer, or free
BREEZY CLOUDY DAY beats fall and spring, but not winter, summer, or free

7. To keep the game going, call for Mother Nature to intervene and all groups split selecting one season, one weather condition, and begin again. Cards that are held in the hand can be used instead of wearing signs.

Energizer 2.37

Pass Matilda Tinklehorn

Number of People: Unlimited

Materials: None

Time: 5 minutes

Directions:

1. This is a variation of the old rumor game.

2. Use the following story about Matilda Tinkelhorn as a rumor to pass from person to person, whispering the short story so as other members don't hear. The last person is to tell what was heard. The group then discusses how accurately the rumor was passed.

   MATILDA TINKLEHORN - Matilda Tinklehorn, who was 93 years old, lived in Tunesville, Tennessee with Tippy her turtle. She also lived with all of her chickens, elephants and koala bears. She enjoyed surfing, except her bathtub was too small and the water kept draining out.

3. A second round can be done with Purple Martians.

   PURPLE MARTIANS - In the year 2042, the Purple Martians from Yukatana came to earth. They were very ugly and had purple faces, 9 arms, 3 heads, 6 ears, bananas for legs and raisins for toes. After landing in San Francisco on the freeway, there was an instant mass of crashes - twelve dozen autos and trucks collided into the green and black 12-pronged spaceship. The Purple Martians were called Polowanos and spoke like they were in echo chambers. Their first words were - "What's Up Doc?"

Energizer 2.38

Hula Hoop Chase

Number of People: 10 - 30

Materials: 2 hula hoops

Time: 10 - 20 minutes

Directions:

1. The group should be divided into two smaller groups.

2. In each group, two people should be designated holders of the hoop, and one member a scorer.

3. The purpose of the activity should be explained to include that the goal of the hula hoop holders is to protect the hoop from invaders.

4. The remaining team members can protect the hoop from the opposite team, remembering that every time an invader enters the hoop, a point is scored for that other team.

5. Keep in mind that the team members must both protect their own hoop and try to enter the other person's hoop.

6. The opposing team B appoints a scorer to stand by team A's hoop and team A appoints a scorer to stand by team B's hoop.

7. There should be some boundaries identified for movement for the group so that it is not impossible to get into the hoop or to protect the hoop.

8. Once a person enters the hoop, that person must stay in the hoop for a period of 10 seconds, at which point no other team member can enter the hoop. That person is then released and goes back to the original team, and must be a protector, until at least one other person has entered the hoop from the opposing team.

9. Play continues until such time as you wish to call time and tally the scores.

Energizer 2.39

Living Picture

Number of People: 15 - 50

Materials: None

Time: 10 - 15 minutes

Directions:

1. The group is divided into four or five smaller groups.
2. There needs to be an open space on the floor area for working.
3. Provide planning time for the groups to coordinate each part of the activity.
4. Instruct the participants that they are going to each have a responsibility in creating a living picture and they will have to work within their groups to finish the picture.
5. The directions for each group can be placed on paper, as well as given orally.
6. Following are the roles and responsibility for each group:

Group I: Build an imaginary frame using the workspace well. As a group, carry a large roll of canvas to the workspace and stretch and tack the canvas to the frame.

Group II: With buckets and brushes, size the piece of canvas in preparation for painting.

Group III: Working as a group, paint a picture on the canvas using all of the space.

Group IV: This group is to be the living part of the picture, therefore they are the characters or the parts of the picture that Group III will use, and when put into position, they are to freeze.

7. Groups I and II should then serve as the critics, evaluating the work of art. Evaluation can be done in writing or nonverbally by showing faces and body posture appropriate to the feelings of the group.

Energizer 2.40

Columbus Discovers America

Number of People: 20 - 30

Materials: Columbus Slips

Time: 10 - 15 minutes

Information:

This particular activity was designed for fourth and fifth graders. Adaptations can be made by increasing the difficulty level and the type of activity or decreasing the difficulty level with fewer instructions and fewer people involved. The slips are not numbered, so that participants are challenged to pick up their cues only from observation. Although this activity is designed for 30, fewer can participate by giving two slips to an individual, being careful to give with additional slips a second one that is not the same as the first, nor one that requires interaction with the first slip. Several of the movements are designed for small groups. The second number is the suggested number that take part.

Directions:

1. Pass out a slip to every participant, making sure that all slips are distributed. Some students may have more than one. Ask the participants to sit in theater style with a stage so that all can observe.

2. The participants are to observe closely what is occurring. You may make this verbal or nonverbal, depending on the intent of the activity, but the participants should observe closely to determine when their part occurs. When they observe an action that cues their participation, they should leave their seats and participate and follow the directions.

3. Listed below are the numbers and the slips that should be distributed. (The second number indicates the number of slips and people to receive slips.)

1-3: You begin. You are a sailor on the Santa Maria. You are scrubbing the deck with a big mop. The sea is very rough, and it is hard to do your job. Empty your mop pail over the side of the rolling ship. Return to your seat.

2-1: After you see sailors mopping the deck of the ship, you are the cook. You are stirring a big pot of fish soup. Wait for others to join you, then give each of them a bowl of the soup. Return to your seat.

3-3: You are a sailor. When you see the cook stirring a big pot of fish soup, join the cook. The cook will give you a bowl of soup. It is not very good. Show that you do not like it very much. Return to your seat.

4-1: You are Christopher Columbus. When you see sailors eating their fish soup, go to the deck and look for land through your spyglass. Show that you do not see land, and walk slowly back to your seat.

5-1: After you see Columbus look for land through his spyglass and return to his seat, you are a sailor looking over the side of the ship. You see something in the water. You are very excited. Motion to others to come to see what you have found. Wait for others to join you, and show them what you have found. Go back to your seat with them.

6-5: When you see someone looking over the side of the ship and motioning to other sailors to come and see, be a sailor and go and see what was found. Crowd around the sailor who found something. Show how happy and excited you feel. Go back to your seat with the others.

7-5: After several sailors have looked at something over the side of the ship, run out on deck and begin working the lines on the sails. Others will help you. Pull hard on the ropes. Go back to the seat with the others.

8-1: You are a sailor. After you have seen other sailors pulling hard on the ropes that work the sails, go on deck and look through your spyglass. You see land. Show the others what you have discovered. Wait for others to join you. When they have, show them the land, and go back to your seat with them.

9-4: You are a sailor. When you see someone point to land, run on deck. Show how excited and happy you are. Look toward the land and show others where it is. Return to your seat.

10-1: After the sailors who are looking and pointing toward land have returned to their seats, be Columbus. Step out of your landing boat. Kneel down on the shore. Stay until you are joined by your sailors. After someone shows a sign to the class, go back to your seat.

11-4: You are a sailor. When you see Columbus step out of a landing boat and kneel down on the shore, join him and kneel down also. Stay until someone shows a sign to the class. Then, go back to your seat.

12-1: When you see Columbus and the sailors kneel down on the shore, while they are still kneeling, show the entire class your sign. Return to your seat. Sign says: "October 12, 1492, Columbus reaches the new world, and you were there!"

Energizer 2.41

Living in a Space Poem

Number of People: Unlimited (most appropriate for elementary age)

Materials: Copy of the poem "Spacesuits," slips of paper with characters on them

Time: 10 minutes

Directions:

1. Explain to the participants that you will be reading a poem to them, and would like for them to listen very carefully to all of the characters and the activities and the kind of space involved for each of the characters.

Poem:

A crack in the sidewalk is plenty of space
For the ants to build their new home.
But the tiger would surely laugh at that place;
He needs a jungle to roam.

Hundreds of honeybees live in a hive,
And the squirrel is content in his trees.
But the eagle requires a piece of the sky,
And the dolphin a part of the seas.

Our pussy is happy to curl up at night,
In a ball, at the foot of my bed,
And the puppy's warm basket fits him just right,
From the tip of his tail to his head.
The leopard, the cougar, the fox and the bear
Need their freedom to range through the wild,
But I know a cozy nook under the stair
That is just the right size for a child.

2. Have slips of paper ready to pass out to participants that have the name of the character or the particular space that will have to be enacted on the designated space in the room, preferably in the middle of a circle. Following the reading of the poem, distribute the slips to the participants.

Characters:

a. Crack in sidewalk   h. Pussycat
b. Ants   i. Puppy
c. Tiger   j. Leopard
d. Honeybees (3)   k. Cougar
e. Squirrel   l. Fox
f. Eagle   m. Bear
g. Dolphin   n. Child

3. On the next reading, the participants are to assume the character as they hear it, all acting as they would within the space designated as read in the poem.

Discussion:

What types of activities were observed? What kind of space was necessary for the various characters for participants? What kind of space is necessary for learning and teaching and exploring?

Energizer 2.42

Tag Variations

Number of People: Unlimited

Materials: None

Time: 10 minutes

Triangle Tag

Directions::

1. Divide into groups of four.

2. Have three people in each group form a triangle by holding hands.

3. Have one of those three people designated as "it."

4. Have the fourth person on the outside of the triangle designated as the chaser.

5. The members of the triangle are to protect "it" from the chaser and when the group is given a signal, the chaser's object is to tag "it."

6. If the "it" target is tagged, the target and the chaser exchange places.

Note:

Tagging should be done on any part other than the hands or arms or from across the triangle.

Partner Tag

Directions::

1. Everyone pairs up with a partner and they must move with their arms interlocked, one right arm to left arm, and "it" is also a pair. "It" must catch another pair and everyone moves. To make it more difficult, the legs are tied together or bagged together, so that it is more difficult to catch people.

2. A variation on partner tag could be triplicate tag, where three people are "it" and must tag other members in groups of three.

Japanese Tag

Directions::

1. One person is designated as "it." When the beat starts (which can be a drum, desktop, or music) everyone moves.

2. As soon as "it" tags another player, that person becomes "it," keeping a hand on the spot where tagged. The next player does the same thing and so on until the end of the game.

3. Players take on a number of different shapes, trying to keep their hands on the tagged spots. They must be innovative to adjust to new body shapes. If a player is tagged a second time, then a second hand is used to touch that part of the body.

"Taper Tom" Tag

Directions::

1. This tag begins the same as Japanese Tag, but one person remains "it" throughout the game.

2. Each person who is tagged comes along with "it," forming a train.

3. Only "it" is allowed to tag another person, and each new addition goes to the end of the line.

Animal Tag

Directions::

1. The players move as whatever animal "it" names. "It" must also be an animal.

2. Each new "it" calls out a new animal.

3. Any player who "it" observes not moving as the animal named automatically becomes "it."

4. "It" may also determine how people are tagged, such as if the animal would be an elephant, then tagging might be with the trunk, which could be an arm or the nose. If the animal was a monkey, the "it" could be tagged with the hand, and so forth.

Energizer 2.43

Catch the Dragon's Tail

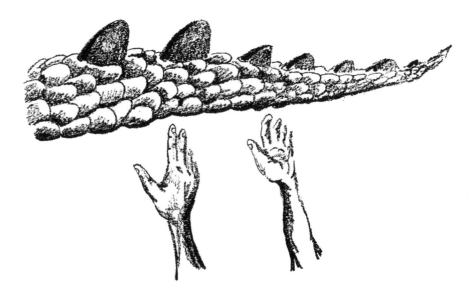

Number of People: Unlimited

Materials: Handkerchief

Time: 5 - 10 minutes

Directions:

1. Participants should be grouped in numbers of 8 - 10 members in a group.

2. The group should form a line with all members lining up one behind the other.

3. The last person in the line tucks a handkerchief in the back of a belt or waistline. To work up steam, the dragon might let out a few roars and puff for smoke.

4. At the signal the dragon begins chasing its own tail and the object for the person at the head of the line is to snatch the handkerchief at the end of the line.

5. When the head grabs the handkerchief, the head then becomes the new tail, while the second from the front becomes the head.

Energizer 2.44
Siamese Relay

Number of People: Unlimited

Materials: Wire hoops or orange cones or markers of some type, cloth strips or string, one ball per team

Time: 10 - 15 minutes

Directions:

1. Set up an obstacle course around which relay teams can maneuver.

2. Use orange cones or wire hoops large enough for a ball to be kicked through, much like a croquet hoop.

3. Relay teams should be divided with approximately 6 to 10 members per team. Team members will pair with another partner and tie their legs together, such as one person's right leg tied to the other person's left leg.

4. The goal of this Siamese relay is for the teams to maneuver the ball around the obstacle course and for the first team to get around before the others.

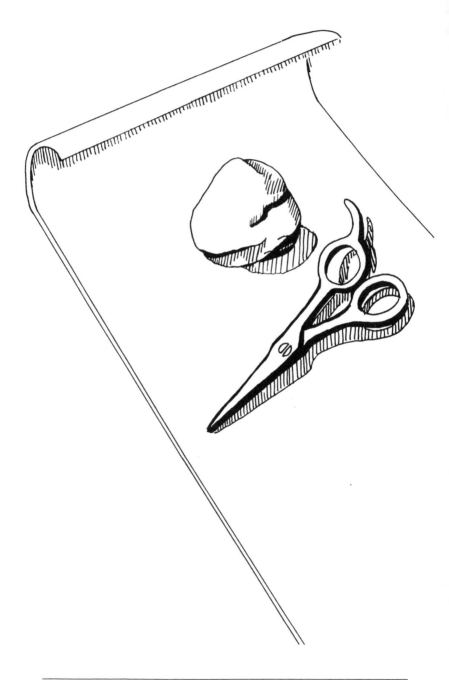

Energizer 2.45

Rock, Paper, Scissors

Number of People: Unlimited

Materials: None

Time: 5 - 15 minutes

Directions::

1. Divide the participants into two groups.

2. Identify a free zone for each team, and a center line over which the two teams can meet.

3. Each team should huddle and collectively decide which symbol they will throw—a rock, paper or scissors. (Just like the old game where paper beats rock by covering it, rock beats scissors by breaking it, and scissors beats paper by cutting it.)

4. In two lines the teams face each other and begin to chant "Rock, Paper, Scissors" and throw their symbols.

5. The team that throws the winning symbol chases the other team, trying to tag as many of their players as possible before they reach their free zone.

6. It is a good idea to have a second choice ready in case of a tie when throwing the rock, paper, or scissors.

7. All tagged players join the team that caught them. This way, teams constantly change numbers and faces and the game keeps going with everyone in it.

Energizer 2.46
Elephant/Palm Tree/Monkey

Number of People: Unlimited

Materials: None

Time: 10 - 15 minutes

Information:

1. "Our jungle world is made of elephants, palm trees and monkeys—each one represented by a three-person pose. An elephant is composed of one person who turns oneself into a long trunk and two other players, one on either side who become large floppy ears. A palm tree has a tall trunk that reaches for the sky, flanked by two arching branches. A monkey always travels in threes and when confronted they assume the classic hear no evil, see no evil, speak no evil pose. Before beginning to play, form a circle and practice making the three characters." The players should learn all three roles that go into each character's pose.

2. This activity begins when one player steps into the center of the circle to be the spinner. The spinner twirls around with a finger pointed outward while the rest of the participants make jungle sounds.

3. The person in the center stops with a finger pointed at one of the participants and calls out the name of one of the characters: elephant, palm tree, or monkey.

4. The person pointed to must assume the central part of that character's pose and the players on either side must complete the picture.

5. All three have to strike the pose before the rest of the group can shout "Elephant, Palm Tree, Monkey."

6. If the group can say "Elephant, Palm Tree, Monkey" before the trio can assume their pose, then the center person takes over as the spinning person in the middle of the circle.

7. If, however, the trio is able to make their pose before the full group says "Elephant, Palm Tree, Monkey," then the person in the center continues in that role until an exchange can be made with another person.

Energizer 2.47

Brainstorming Contest

Number of People: Unlimited

Materials: An example of whatever is going to be brainstormed, such as paper clip, comb, or ruler

Time: 10 minutes

Directions:

1. Explain to the group that this is a contest, and the groups will attempt to brainstorm as many different ways to use the object that you hold up as possible. There will be 4-6 members per group.

2. Instruct the groups to identify a recorder who will write down all suggestions.

3. The object that is chosen should be the same for each group.

4. Select items from the following list and allow approximately 3-5 minutes for the groups to brainstorm: pine cone, toothpick, candle, rule, paper clip, scissors, pencil, push pin, balloon, rubber band, barrette, bobby pin, nail, screw, hammer, spoon, knife, hair ribbon, pencil, pencil sharpener, chair, eraser, penny, sock, paper, button, saucer, dog bone, and feather.

5. Have the recorder or another member of the group read the brainstormed list at the conclusion of the time period allotted. Repeat the procedure with a different item.

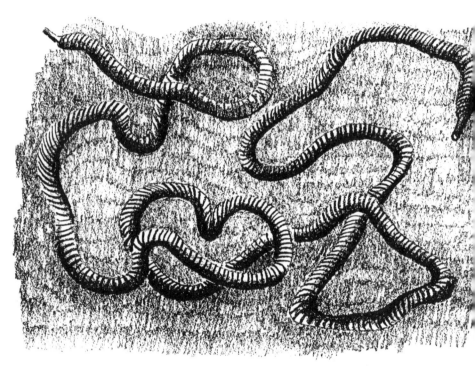

Energizer 2.48

String Maze

Number of People: Unlimited

Materials: Ball of string or yarn

Time: 10 minutes

Directions:

1. The participants should be instructed to form a circle.

2. A volunteer should stand in the center of the circle.

3. A ball of string will be given to one member of the circle, and members will be instructed to create a maze around the person in the center. The ball of string will be passed and/or thrown from one member to the next without directly crossing over the person in the center. The only other rule is that it cannot be passed either directly to the right or the left of the person holding the string.

4. After approximately three minutes of creating the string maze, the participants are then instructed to undo the maze by accurately throwing to the person who holds the string and this is done as the person in the center directs the participants where to throw the string.

Energizer 2.49
Sentence Bee

Number of People: 13 - 52

Materials: Two packs of cards with words on the individual cards

Time: 15 minutes

Directions:

1. One set of words should be placed on 5 x 7 cards or 8 1/2 x 11 sheets of paper all in the same color. Example: all in red. Another set of words should be placed on an identical sized card or piece of paper in a different color. Example: all in black.

   Following are words to be used:

   full, ideas, good, nice, cooperative, feels, helps, helping, others, way, know, yourself, better, and, through, friend, special, exciting, one, who, it, in, be, the, of, a, to, is, can,

2. Each participant should receive one word or each participant should receive enough words on their team to insure that a sentence could be created. A period, comma, or exclamation mark should be added if there are a few extra people. Teams would consist of 13 - 26 per side.

3. Call out in random order the words from one of the sentences below. The words should not be in a sequence that would make sense. The numbers in parenthesis are point values.

   1. To be full of ideas is good. (7)
   2. It is nice to be cooperative. (6)
   3. It feels good to exchange ideas. (6)
   4. Helping others is a way to know yourself better. (9)
   5. Be nice and be good. (5)
   6. Helping others feels good. (4)
   7. A way to know yourself is through helping others.(9)
   8. It is nice to be a friend. (7)
   9. A friend helping others is special. (6)
   10. Special ideas can be exciting. (5)
   11. A helping friend is special. (5)
   12. A special friend is one who helps others. (8)

4. The people with those words should come forward and form a sentence.

5. The side forming a sentence first gets the points that each sentence is worth. If a sentence other than the line listed is created, that sentence is acceptable as well. The point value, however, would remain the same. It is a good idea to have a time limit.

6. At the conclusion of the time allotted for the activity, the points are totaled.

Variation: The same thing can be done with the alphabet, by spelling individual words and having students hold letters and come forward to spell words.

Energizer 2.50
Second Look

Number of People: Unlimited

Materials: None

Time: 10 minutes

Directions:

1. Ask the participants to sit in a circle.

2. Ask for 3 - 4 volunteers who will be the first observers.

3. Ask the observers to stand in the center of the circle and to spend approximately one minute looking at various members of the group.

4. The observers will then leave the room, while the group all makes a particular change, either in the way they had their knees crossed, their arms crossed, buttons buttoned, but the initial change will be for the entire group.

5. The volunteers come back and stand in the circle and attempt to locate the change that the group made. They have a maximum of three guesses. Once they are able to guess what change took place, then they select someone to exchange places with, and four more observers stand in the center.

6. After three to four times of the group making a change, the next level of difficulty is for the observers to go out and only four people in the group make a change. Therefore, the observing time is critical.

7. The observers return, trying to locate the four people who made a specific change. At this point, the four members may either make the same kind of change or the four members may each make a different change from the other member.

8. After three times in this fashion, reverse the process, by having the volunteers go out of the room and make a change on themselves, and return to the center, with the group identifying what the change was. Whoever is able to identify the change first, exchanges with the person in the center.

Energizer 2.51
The Backside Shuffle

Number of People: Unlimited

Materials: Balloon, string, and a whistle

Time: 5 - 10 minutes

Directions:

1. The participants should be given pieces of string long enough to wrap around each waist and attach to a balloon.

2. Each participant should blow up a balloon, tie it to the string and then tie the string around the waist with about 3 - 4" extra string length.

3. Divide the participants into groups of 6 to 8.

4. At the whistle, members of the group are to sit on their other member's balloon—not their own, just other team members.

5. The first group to pop all of their balloons is the winner.

6. No hands or feet can be used to pop the balloons.

Bibliography

Cottrell, J. (1975). *Teaching with creative dramatics.* Skokie, IL: National Textbook Company.

Foster, E.S. (1983). *Tutoring: Learning by helping.* Minneapolis, MN: Educational Media Corporation.

Fleugelman, A. ed. (1976). *The new games book.* Tiburon, CA: Headlands Press.

Fleugelman, A. ed. (1981). *More new games!.* Tiburon, CA: Headlands Press.

Mill, C. (1980). *Activities for trainers: 50 useful designs.* San Diego, CA: University Associates, Inc.

Pfeiffer, J.W. and Jones, J.E. (1973). *A handbook of structured experiences for human relations training,* Vol. IV. San Diego, CA: University Associates, Inc.

Pfeiffer, J.W. and Jones, J.E. (1980). *The 1980 handbook for group facilitators.* San Diego, CA: University Associates, Inc.

Pfeiffer, J.W. and Jones, J. E. (1981). *A handbook of structured experiences for human relations training,* Vol VIII. San Diego, CA: University Associates, Inc.

Acknowledgements

Permission has been granted for the following activities to be included in this collection. It is with great appreciation that I cite these particular references.

1.2 Name Switching—Reprinted from: J. William Pfeiffer and John E. Jones (eds.), *A Handbook of Structured Experiences for Human Relations Training*, Vol. VIII. San Diego, CA: University Associates, Inc., 1981, pp. 5-6. (Used with permission.)

1.13 Hometown Map—Reprinted from: J. William Pfeiffer and John E. Jones (eds.), *A Handbook of Structured Experiences for Human Relations Training*, Vol. IV. San Diego, CA: University Associates, Inc., 1973, p. 3. (Used with permission.)

1.27 Autographs—Reprinted from: J. William Pfeiffer and John E. Jones (eds.) *The 1980 Annual Handbook for Group Facilitators.* San Diego, CA: University Associates, Inc., 1973, p. 3. (Used with permission.)

2.7 The Numbers Game—Reprinted from: C. Mill. *Activities for Training: 50 Useful Designs.* San Diego, CA: University Associates, Inc., 1980, pp. 14-16. (Used with permission.)

2.40 Columbus Discovers America—Reprinted from: J. Cottrell. *Teaching with Creative Dramatics.* Skokie, IL: National Textbook Company, 1975, pp. 78-80. (Used with permission.)

2.41 Living in a Space Poem—Reprinted from J. Cottrell. *Teaching with Creative Dramatics*, Skokie, IL: National Textbook Company, 1975. (Used with permission.)

2.42 Tag Variations—Reprinted from J. Cottrell. *Teaching with Creative Dramatics.* Skokie, IL: National Textbook Company, 1975, pp. 131-132. (Used with permission.)

2.51 Second Look—Reprinted from J. Cottrell. *Teaching with Creative Dramatics.* Skokie, IL: National Textbook Company, 1975, p. 75. (Used with permission.)

2.43 Catch the Dragon's Tail, 2.44 Rock, Paper, Scissors from A. Fluegelman. (ed.). (1976). *The New Games Book.* Tiburon, CA: Headlands Press. (Reprinted by permission of Doubleday, a division of Bantam, Doubleday, Dell Publishing Group, Inc.)

2.42 Triangle Tag, 2.46 Elephant, Palm Tree, Monkey from A. Fluegelman. (1981). *More New Games!* Tiburon, CA: Headlands Press. (Reprinted by permission of Doubleday, a division of Bantam, Doubleday, Dell Publishing Group, Inc.)